Healthy Beginnings, Healthy Futures

A Judge's Guide

ABA Center on Children and the Law
Eva J. Klain, JD
Lisa Pilnik, JD, MS
Erin Talati, JD, MD

National Council of Juvenile and Family Court Judges
Candice L. Maze, JD

Zero to Three National Policy Center
Kimberly Diamond-Berry, PhD
Lucy Hudson, MS

Edited by Claire S. Chiamulera

This judge's guide was supported in full by Grant #G96MC04451, Improving Understanding of Maternal and Child Health, to the American Bar Association 's Center on Children and the Law from the U.S. Department of Health and Human Services, Health Resources and Services Administration, Maternal and Child Health Bureau.

The views expressed herein are those of the authors and have not been approved by the House of Delegates or the Board of Governors of the American Bar Association or by the U.S. Department of Health and Human Services and, accordingly, should not be viewed as representing the policy of the ABA or DHHS.

Cover design by ABA Publishing. Page design by Zaccarine Design, Inc., Evanston, IL
Index prepared by Mertes Editorial Services, Alexandria, VA

Library of Congress Cataloging-in-Publication Data

Healthy beginnings, healthy futures : a judge's guide / Eva J. Klain
...[et al.] ; edited by Claire S. Chiamulera.
    p. cm.
  Includes bibliographical references and index.
  ISBN 978-1-60442-611-3 (alk. paper)
 1. Children--Legal status, laws, etc.--United States. 2.
Children--Health and hygiene--United States. I. Klain, Eva J., 1964-
II. Sandt, Claire.
  KF3735.H43 2009
  344.7303'219892--dc22
                              2009033427

Contents

Foreword

Janet, who just turned 18 last week, is on the phone for a shelter hearing from the Birthing Center at the hospital. She had her first baby, Mariah, yesterday. Janet is crying hard. The state wants to place Mariah in foster care. The state says Janet is unstable, has used methamphetamine in the past, and is too immature to safely parent. The state explains that Janet was abused and neglected as an infant. She grew up in foster care, in numerous placements, and was, until recently, an out-of-control teenager. Janet says she has put that past behind her. She has her own apartment. She is clean now and the baby was born clean. She says she wants the chance to parent her baby because she wants a family, her own family, something she never had.

The judge considers: What can be done to help Janet be a successful parent? How can the judge give her a chance without risking that the same thing happens to her child as happened to her? And if foster care occurs, what can the judge do to ensure the baby is not injured further by being a ward of the court?

Judges make decisions like this every day. On average, infants and toddlers comprise about one third of our national abuse and neglect caseload. Infants and toddlers—our most vulnerable and precious wards—present an opportunity for judges to do the most harm or to provide the most help. The science of early child development now gives us a clear understanding of the ways we can improve developmental outcomes for infants and toddlers at a time when the rapid rate of brain development provides the best chance for effective intervention. If we know the science and act on it, we can ensure healthy growth and development. This guide gives us those tools. This guide gives us the science in one comprehensive volume so we can usher in a new way to do business when it comes to infants and toddlers in dependency court.

We need a new way to do business. Very young children develop within the context of their primary relationships. They are hurt and healed within that context. Science teaches us that the quality and reliability of those first relationships forms the actual physical architecture of the baby's brain. Since first relationships are primary, we must take a relational approach to case planning for infants and toddlers, by helping parents learn how to have a reciprocal loving relationship with their child. Since first relationships are primary, we must not allow multiple placements of infants and toddlers and find more permanent placements sooner. Since first relationships are primary, we must reframe visitation. Visitation should be a therapeutic opportunity to promote, enhance, and shape the bond between parent and child and not just a "right" of the parent to spend time with the child.

This guide helps ensure that as a nation, we equip the bench to do better by babies every day. Judges can be key players in breaking the intergenerational cycle of abuse and neglect. Read the guide and pass it along to a fellow judge. Push for a relational approach in every case. Let's act now. Let's usher in a new future now, one baby at a time. Mariah—and Janet—can't wait.

Judge Pamela L. Abernethy
Marion County Circuit Court
Salem, Oregon

Preface

A recent explosion of research on early brain development highlights how crucial the early years are in the health and development of infants, toddlers, and preschoolers. The foundation laid early in life affects their childhoods, adolescence, and adult lives. This very young population is especially vulnerable to the effects of abuse and neglect that set the stage for their long-term health outcomes.

As legal professionals dedicated to the safety and well-being of children in foster care, it is important to educate ourselves not just about the laws and regulations that govern what happens in the courtroom, but also learn from other disciplines about the health needs of this population. Safe, permanent homes for very young children must also mean healthy attachment to nurturing families and caregivers, up-to-date immunizations, a medical home, and comprehensive oral health care.

This guide provides you, in one easily accessible resource, a comprehensive source of information about the health needs of very young children in care within the context of permanency decision-making. We hope it will help you ask the right questions, require the necessary health-related information, and make the life-altering decisions that meet the unique health needs of very young children in the child welfare system.

You can promote the health of the infants, toddlers, and preschoolers who come before you in the courtroom and help them achieve their full potential. Their healthy beginnings can lead to healthy futures.

Eva J. Klain

Acknowledgements

There are many people without whom this judge's guide would not be possible. The authors would like to thank the members of the ABA Center on Children and the Law's Improving Understanding of Maternal and Child Health (IUMCH) project advisory committee for their staunch support of this endeavor and for all their time and efforts in reviewing drafts of the manuscript. Their invaluable guidance and wealth of knowledge and experience in responding to the health needs of court-involved infants, toddlers, and preschoolers enriched the content.

We are grateful for the support of the leadership and staff of the three organizations that partnered to develop this guide. The ABA Center on Children and the Law, the National Council of Juvenile and Family Court Judges, and the Zero to Three Policy Center each brought diverse expertise and unique insights to the project, ensuring its broad coverage and interdisciplinary perspective.

We are especially grateful to Moira Szilagyi, MD, who lent her extensive knowledge of the medical needs of children in foster care to the physical health chapter. Special thanks also to Jessie Buerlein and Burton L. Edelstein, DDS, of the Children's Dental Health Project for their careful review and contributions to the section on dental homes and dental care for very young children.

Thanks to ABA Center intern Allison Green for her research, cite checking and overall support.

Thanks also to Audrey Yowell, our federal project officer, for her unwavering support, insights, and encouragement throughout the development of this guide. And thank you to our Alliance for Information on Maternal and Child Health (AIM) partners who reviewed various chapters and provided valuable feedback.

And finally, a special thank you to Claire Chiamulera for her extraordinary editing talents, constant support, and timely encouragement. Claire's substantial guidance throughout the development of this guide ensured its comprehensiveness and accessibility.

Advisory Committee

The Honorable Pamela L. Abernethy
Marion County Circuit Court
Salem, OR

Jessie Buerlein, MSW
Children's Dental Health Project
Washington, DC

The Honorable Constance Cohen
Polk County Juvenile Court
Des Moines, IA

Sheryl Dicker, JD
Albert Einstein College of Medicine
New York, NY

The Honorable Stephanie Domitrovich
Erie County Juvenile Court
Erie, PA

Mary R. Haack, PhD, RN, FAAN
University of Maryland
School of Nursing
Baltimore, MD

Sheri L. Hill, PhD
Early Childhood Policy Specialist
Seattle, WA

Brenda Jones Harden, PhD
Institute for Child Study,
University of Maryland
College Park, MD

Anne Kellogg, JD
National Association of
Counsel for Children
Denver, CO

The Honorable Cindy S. Lederman
11th Judicial Circuit of Florida
Miami, FL

The Honorable Katherine Lucero
Superior Court, Santa Clara County
San Jose, CA

Candice L. Maze, JD
Maze Consulting, Inc.
Miami, FL

Joy D. Osofsky, PhD
Louisiana State University
Health Sciences Center
New Orleans, LA

JoAnne Solchany, PhD
Seattle University
University of Washington
Bothell, WA

Kelly Towey, MEd
Parent Education Consultant
Downers Grove, IL

Understanding Federal Laws and Programs

The following federal laws and grant programs support judges' efforts to meet the health care needs of very young children in foster care.

Medicaid

The Medicaid program is jointly funded by the federal and state governments and administered by states according to federal guidelines. Most foster children can receive Medicaid because program requirements are tied to eligibility for state reimbursement for foster care expenses under Title IV-E of the Social Security Act. The federal government requires that "mandatory" services, such as physician and hospital services, family planning, and laboratory and x-ray services be included in all states' Medicaid programs, while other, "optional" services, such as prescription drugs, vision, dental, home-based care, and physical therapy may be included if a state chooses.[1]

Under the Early and Periodic Screening, Diagnosis and Treatment (EPSDT) provisions of Medicaid, however, *children* are entitled to all of the services in the federal law's "optional" list, whether or not the state chooses to offer those benefits to adults.[2] EPSDT requires that state Medicaid programs provide a comprehensive set of screening, diagnosis, and treatment services to children under age 21 enrolled in Medicaid. This includes periodic screenings at established age-appropriate intervals for mental and physical health issues, as well as additional screenings if a problem is suspected. The screening component "includes a comprehensive health and developmental history, an unclothed physical exam, appropriate immunizations, laboratory tests, and health education."[3] Despite the broad reach of this benefit, studies show it is underused, causing many children's health needs to go unidentified. Courts can ensure that such services are provided to children in care by routinely asking about screening results.

Two services available for children under EPSDT may be particularly helpful for children in foster care:

- **Targeted Case Management (TCM):** Thirty-eight states use TCM services to provide coordinated care and access to needed medical services for children in foster care.[4] Using these case management services makes it more likely for children to receive physician, prescription drug, hospitalization, rehabilitative, and mental health services than those who do not receive TCM.[5] In states where TCM is used, judges should routinely ask if TCM is being provided for children in care.

- **Rehabilitative Services:** Rehabilitative services may include services to reduce physical or mental disabilities and ensure optimal functioning. The services can also include certain specialized placements including therapeutic foster care and other family support services that improve children's functioning. This option is sometimes used to permit a child in care to remain in the least restrictive setting while receiving essential mental health services.

Children's Health Insurance Program (CHIP)

Through the 2009 Children's Health Insurance Program Reauthorization Act (CHIPRA),[6] CHIP continues to provide health insurance to low-income children whose families earn too much to qualify for Medicaid.[7] In combination with Medicaid, CHIP aims to decrease the number of uninsured children. The program is an essential source of health insurance for children in the child welfare system who are not eligible for Medicaid or who are transitioning out of care and therefore losing their eligibility for Medicaid. Judges should ensure that foster children will have health insurance when they are no longer in care by requiring that caseworkers and reunifying or adoptive families address this issue while the child is still under the court's jurisdiction.

Title V Maternal and Child Health Block Grant to States Program

This program provides funding for a range of health-related services, such as respite care for families caring for special needs children, or outreach to educate low-income families about food stamps.[8] States have wide discretion on what to fund with these grants. Some families in your court may benefit from services your state has chosen—check with your state's Title V director. (A list is available at https://perfdata.hrsa.gov/mchb/mchreports/link/state_links.asp.)

Healthy Start

Healthy Start grants fund local programs that address infant mortality, low birthweight, and racial disparities in infant health. Services offered include case management to help families access health care and other resources, peer mentoring for parents, and postpartum depression screening. Efforts are also made to connect families to other services to address their specific issues, including housing or employment barriers, substance abuse, domestic violence, or mental health problems. Encourage caseworkers, attorneys and families to look into the services offered by a local Healthy Start program for infants and/or pregnant women. For more information and to access a list of local programs, visit www.healthystartassoc.org/ and click on "Directory."

Health Insurance Portability and Accountability Act (HIPAA)[9]

Enacted in 1996, HIPAA prevents the use or disclosure of protected health information (PHI) by certain entities, including child welfare agencies *if* they are considered health care providers. (The Department of Health and Human Services provides a tool to determine when an entity is a health care provider at www.cms.hhs.gov/apps/hipaa2decisionsupport/.) PHI includes any health information that could reasonably be used to identify an individual.

Several exceptions may apply in child welfare proceedings, however. PHI may be used or disclosed when:

- reporting abuse or neglect; and
- the information relates to judicial or administrative proceedings if the request is made through a court order or administrative tribunal.

The exceptions under HIPAA provide for sharing of information between the child welfare agency, courts, and health providers for children, although questions still remain about its application in practice, including the ability of parents to access the records of their children in care.[10] Respecting the privacy rights of even the youngest children in care now can protect them against future discrimination.

Child Abuse Prevention and Treatment Act (CAPTA)/Individuals with Disabilities Education Act (IDEA) Part C

CAPTA requires that states refer children under age three who have a substantiated case of child abuse or neglect for screening for early intervention services funded by Part C of IDEA.[11] This federal grant program helps states implement a comprehensive system for early intervention referrals and services. States have some discretion in setting evaluation criteria, therefore eligibility definitions vary significantly from state to state. Once a child is deemed eligible for early intervention services, an Individual Family Services Plan (IFSP) must be developed within 45 days of referral.[12] IDEA Part C can help ensure that very young children's developmental needs are met through services such as occupational and speech therapies, counseling, nursing services, transportation, and more. Ask if each infant and toddler in your courtroom has been evaluated and has received recommended services.

Fostering Connections to Success and Increasing Adoptions Act of 2008 (Fostering Connections Act)[13]

The Fostering Connections Act addresses many issues that promote permanency and affect the health and well-being of very young children in foster care, including:

- making it easier for relatives to care for children;
- increasing adoption incentives and support;
- increasing resources that help birth families stay together or reunite;
- placing greater priority on keeping siblings together;
- helping students stay in the same school or promptly transfer when they enter care;
- providing more direct support to American Indian and Alaskan Native children; and
- increasing support for training of staff working with children in the child welfare system.

The Fostering Connections Act also requires states to develop plans to coordinate and oversee health services for children in foster care, in consultation with health care and child welfare experts. Each state's plan must include a coordinated strategy to identify and respond to children's health care needs, including mental and dental health.

State plans must address:

- schedules for health screenings;
- monitoring and treatment of identified needs;
- sharing and updating of health records;
- continuity of care;
- monitoring of prescription medications; and
- collaboration between the state and health professionals for assessment and treatment of health issues.

Endnotes

1. *Medicare: A Primer.* Menlo Park, CA: The Henry J. Kaiser Family Foundation, January 2009. Available at www.kff.org/medicaid/upload/7334-03.pdf.

2. Ibid.

3. *EPSDT Program Background.* Rockville, MD: Health Resources and Services Administration. Available at www.hrsa.gov/epsdt/overview.htm#1.

4. Geen, R., A. Sommers and M. Cohen. "Medicaid Spending on Foster Children." Urban Institute Child Welfare Research Program, Brief No. 2, August 2005. Available at www.urban.org/Uploaded PDF/311221_medicaid_spending.pdf.

5. Ibid.

6. P.L. 111-3.

7. Klain, E. "What Passage of CHIPRA Means for Child Advocates." *Child Law Practice* 28(1), March 2009, 12.

8. *Block Grant Program.* Rockville, MD: Health Resources and Services Administration, Maternal and Child Health Bureau. Available at https://perfdata.hrsa.gov/mchb/mchreports/ LEARN_More/Block_Grant_Program/block_grant_program.asp.

9. P.L. 104-191.

10. Klain, E. "Federal Confidentiality Laws and Dependency Courts: Managing Competing Interests." *The Judges' Page Newsletter*, February 2006. Available at www.nationalcasa.org/ download/Judges_Page/0602_mental_health_issue_0036.pdf.

11. U.S. Department of Health and Human Services, Administration for Children and Families. *Child Welfare Policy Manual.* Available at www.acf.hhs.gov/j2ee/programs/cb/laws_policies/ laws/cwpm/policy_dsp.jsp?citID=354. 20 U.S.C.A. § 1437.

12. Child Welfare Information Gateway. *Addressing the Needs of Young Children in Child Welfare: Part C—Early Intervention Services*, 2007. Available at www.childwelfare.gov/ pubs/partc/partc_a.cfm.

13. P.L. 110-351.

chapter 1

Meeting the Needs of Very Young Children in Dependency Court

Early experiences and relationships significantly impact a child's development.[1] From birth to five years old, children develop the foundation for their future linguistic, cognitive, emotional, social, regulatory and moral capabilities.[2] The science of early child development clearly shows the importance of parenting and regular, consistent caregiving to a child's healthy growth and development.[3] The health and well-being of children's parents or primary caregivers are also crucial to a child's early development.[4]

The growth and development of very young children are profoundly affected by abuse, neglect and removal. As the largest group to enter the child welfare system, very young children who become the subject of dependency court proceedings face multiple disadvantages, traumas, and losses during a critical time of early brain development.

As a judge who handles child welfare cases, the cumulative effect of harmful early life experiences likely challenges your efforts to seek positive developmental and permanency outcomes for children birth through five years old. However, this stage of development can also provide opportunities to intervene early and pursue strategies to clear the path for healthy growth and development. You can take advantage of this opportunity by collaborating with health care professionals, child welfare workers, and others to implement proven interventions and use science to inform your decision making.

How Very Young Children Experience the Child Welfare System

Age is strongly associated with (1) the likelihood of a child entering the child welfare system; (2) how long children remain in out-of-home placements; (3) how children exit the system; and (4) the likelihood of reentry.[6] Even considering other factors such as economics, policy, administrative structure, and method of service delivery, age largely determines what happens to children in foster care.[7]

A baby's social-emotional development, specifically attachment to a primary caregiver, is affected by removal from his parent and multiple placements while in care.[8] Research shows that young children, even newborns and infants, experience long-lasting sadness, grief, loss, and rejection.[9] Separations occurring between six months and approximately three years of age are even more likely to cause later emotional disturbances.[10] These findings stress the need to consider the social-emotional development of very young children when making judicial decisions about removal, placement, and permanency.

Key Terms

▸ **Very young children** and **infants, toddlers, and preschoolers**: used interchangeably to describe children from birth through age five

▸ **Infants**: children from birth to one year old

▸ **Toddlers**: children between the ages of one and three years old

▸ **Preschoolers**: children ages three through five

▸ **Court-involved children**, **dependent children**, and **children in care**: very young children under the jurisdiction of a judge or court system that oversees dependency matters (civil child welfare proceedings), irrespective of a child's physical placement.[5] This book applies to all infants, toddlers, and preschoolers who are or have been the subject of a dependency petition, whether they are living with their biological parents, relatives, nonrelatives, or in a licensed foster home or group home.

▸ **Foster caregivers and foster parents**: includes kinship caregivers and relative and nonrelative caregivers

Entering Care

Of the 311,000 children who entered care across the United States in 2005, those from birth through five years old represented 38% of new admissions.[11] This was largely because 15%, or 46,954, of the new admissions were infants less than one year of age.[12] More recently, a national study found that 91,278 babies in the United States under age one were victims of nonfatal child abuse or neglect between October 2005 and September 2006.[13] Of these babies, 29,881 were victims of neglect (70%) or physical abuse (13%) before they reached *one week* of age.[14]

Very young children who enter the child welfare system are disproportionately children of color. Although African American children make up only 15% of the U.S. population of children, they represent approximately 37% of the children in the system.[15] In 2005, the placement rate of infants in foster care was 18.8 for every 1,000 African American children in the United States.[16]

A primary reason that very young children enter care is identified maternal drug and alcohol abuse.[17] This is especially true for newborns identified as exposed to drugs or alcohol through a toxicology report in the hospital.[18] Increased reporting and economic pressures facing families may also contribute to the high number of very young children entering care. Our ever younger child population overall, as well as wider use of early interventions, are likely related to the influx of infants, toddlers, and preschoolers into the child welfare system.[19]

Time in Out-of-Home Care

Once removed from homes and placed in foster care, infants and toddlers are more likely to stay in foster care for more than one year.[20] According to the 2006 Adoption and Foster Care Analysis and Reporting System (AFCARS) report for fiscal year 2005, of those children with a goal of adoption and/or whose parental rights had been terminated, 59% entered care at age five or younger.[21] Of the 59% of children 'waiting' for adoption as of September 30, 2005, 23% had entered care before their first birthday.[22] Another study underscored the challenges facing these 'waiting' children, finding that 50% of the children who were first placed as infants with a permanency plan of adoption took more than 39 months to be adopted, with nearly 17 of the 39 months accruing *after* becoming legally free for adoption.[23]

Challenges for Very Young Children in Out-of-Home Care

Because of their exposure to conditions that are not conducive to healthy development, many very young children in care have a mixture of physical, developmental, and emotional challenges. Factors such as low birth weight and lack of prenatal care are closely related to long stays in care.[24] These deficits often cause the child to have multiple needs that may complicate attaining positive and permanent placements. Additionally, infants and toddlers are more likely to be neglected and abused while in care than older children, especially babies who enter care between birth and three months of age.[25]

Exits from the Child Welfare System

Although the probability of adoption is much higher for children entering out-of-home care before their first birthday than for older children, the likelihood for reunification is much lower.[26] Only 36% of infants who enter care between birth and three months of age are reunified with their parents, and 56% of infants who enter care between 10-12 months of age are reunified with their parents.[27] Poor reunification rates for the very youngest children partly relate to the physical, emotional and/or developmental needs resulting from limited prenatal care, unhealthy living situations or abuse and neglect.[28] Also, because substance abuse is common among mothers of very young children in care, many addicted parents cannot become clean and sober within the constraints of the Adoption and Safe Families Act's (ASFA) timelines.

As with entry into foster care, disproportionality is evident when looking at exits of children of color from foster care. Like older children of color in care, very young children of color spend longer periods in care than their white counterparts and are less likely to be adopted once parental rights are terminated.[29]

Reentry

One-third of infants discharged from the child welfare system reenter care.[30] Evidence shows that infants who return to foster care experience much longer stays in care upon their return.[31] Reentry rates for infants discharged to relatives are lower than those for infants reunified with biological parents (this is also true for older children).[32]

How the Bench Can Make an Impact

Courts, in partnership with multiple systems, can reduce the number of very young children in out-of-home placements and minimize the effects of maltreatment and removal on their development. As the judge, understanding the unique needs of young maltreated children can help you ensure their needs are met on all levels (developmental, physical health, mental health) by promoting appropriate screening, assessments and interventions; ensuring regular contact with biological families; making appropriate placements; and expediting permanency.

By understanding how health, early child development, attachment, placement and safety interrelate, you can better promote positive and permanent outcomes for very young children. This is a compelling endeavor because decisions in dependency court often influence whether a baby develops into a securely attached, healthy, well-functioning child, or takes a different course in her development.

Many judges across the country have taken the lead in elevating the needs of babies, toddlers, and preschoolers in their jurisdictions through court-run projects, interventions, publications and collaborative models. The elements that underlie the success of these efforts are detailed in the final chapter of this book. By incorporating them into daily practice judges can shape policies and practices that identify and address the multifaceted needs of very young children in care.

This book serves as your guide to the wide array of health needs of very young children in care. By sharing current research on physical health, child development, attachment, infant mental health, and early care and education, the authors provide tools and strategies to help you promote better outcomes for babies, toddlers, and preschoolers who enter your courtroom. Specific goals are to:

- Underscore the sense of urgency for the youngest children in care and build consensus among judges who work with this population that a special focus is necessary to ensure the child protection system and courts take care of these vulnerable children.
- Synthesize extensive research about young children in general and specific research related to young children in care that apply to judges' daily decision making.

- Provide strength-based, holistic tools and techniques to support judges in achieving positive outcomes for this population, including strategies to reduce the harm caused by removal and long stays in care, and mediate the impact of maltreatment and resulting developmental delays and impairments.
- Offer information about evidence-based programs and interventions that can aid judges and other child welfare professionals in building community-based supports for very young children.

How This Book Is Organized

Entire volumes are devoted to the topics presented in the following chapters. Reducing decades of research and practice into a succinct and useful resource is challenging. Moreover, human development is complex and influenced by many factors. Genetics, environment, trauma, and support systems impact each other and interact with overall child development and well-being. Discussing attachment and mental health independently from physical health and development for very young children presents logistical challenges, which become more complex when the child has been maltreated and exposed to multiple caregivers and environments. Thus, while divided into discrete topical chapters, this book should be viewed as an integrated resource for making decisions for very young children under the jurisdiction of the dependency court.

- **Chapter 2 examines physical health needs** of infants, toddlers and preschoolers as well as special health-related considerations for very young children under dependency court jurisdiction. Special health needs and medical issues that arise for these children are explored. Comprehensive health assessments, specific health-related screenings, and immunizations are reviewed.

- **Chapter 3 examines mental health and developmental needs** of very young children in care within the context of essential relationships. This chapter discusses the very young child's social-emotional development, the basic need for secure and stable attachments, and the impact of trauma on the mental health of the very young child in dependency court. The cognitive and developmental needs of infants, toddlers, and preschoolers in care are described, with a focus on screening and intervention to address and prevent delays. The chapter shares practices that support the healthy cognitive and social-emotional development of very young children in dependency court.

This chapter also **explores early care and education settings** for infants, toddlers and preschoolers in the child welfare system. Many very young children involved with the dependency court process are not only in out-of-home living arrangements, but also in child care centers, family group care settings, or early education programs such as Early Head Start/Head Start and prekindergarten programs. This chapter describes these programs, discusses the importance of quality early care environments, and examines the potential added value these settings may have in the developmental process of a very young child in care.

- **Chapter 4 focuses on permanency planning strategies and postpermanency supports** for very young children. It places the information in the preceding chapters into the context of the dependency court process and the overarching systemic goal of timely permanency for very young children in care. This chapter uses the *RESOURCE GUIDELINES: Improving Court Practice in Child Abuse and Neglect Cases*[33] as a framework for discussing key decisions for infants, toddlers, and preschoolers at each required hearing. A significant portion of Chapter 4 discusses permanency outcomes and options from a very young child's perspective and strategies for preventing postpermanency reentry into care.

- **Chapter 5 concludes with a brief Call to Action** for judges and other child welfare system partners to explore and make meaningful systemic changes for very young children in care. It focuses on judges as change agents who can advance policies and interventions that minimize the harm to young children of long stays in care and support their healthy development while under the jurisdiction of the dependency court.

Endnotes

1. Shonkoff, J.P. and D.A. Phillips, eds. *From Neurons to Neighborhoods: The Science of Early Childhood Development*. National Research Council and Institute of Medicine Committee on Integrating the Science of Early Childhood Development. Washington, D.C.: National Academy Press, 2000, 1-2.

2. Ibid., 5.

3. Ibid., 7.

4. Ibid.

5. Recognizing that many family courts and courts of general jurisdiction oversee child welfare proceedings, 'dependency court' is used to refer to children under the jurisdiction of any court or judge authorized to hear civil cases involving child maltreatment or abandonment.

6. Wulczyn, F., K.B. Hislop and B. Jones Harden. "The Placement of Infants in Foster Care." *Infant Mental Health Journal* 23(5), 2002, 463.

7. Ibid.

8. Wulczyn, Hislop and Jones Harden, 2002, 454-475, 457.

9. Shonkoff and Phillips, 2000, 28.

10. Cohen, J. and V. Youcha. "Zero to Three: Critical Issues for the Juvenile and Family Court." *Juvenile and Family Court Journal* 17, Spring 2004, 15-28.

11. U.S. Department of Health and Human Services, Administration for Children and Families. *The AFCARS Report*. Washington, D.C.: Administration on Children, Youth and Families, Children's Bureau, 2006. Available at www.acf.hhs.gov/programs/cb.

12. Ibid.

13. 905,000 children in the U.S. during this period had substantiated allegations of maltreatment, thus infants, those under one year of age, represented 19% of the total number of children.

14. Centers for Disease Control and Prevention. "Nonfatal Maltreatment of Infants – United States, October 2005 – September 2006." *Morbidity and Mortality Weekly Report* 57(13), 336-339, April 2008. Available at www.cdc.gov/mmwr/preview/mmwrhtml/mm5713a2.htm.

15. Wulczyn, F. and B. Lery. *Racial Disparity in Foster Care Admissions*. Chicago: Chapin Hall Center for Children at the University of Chicago, September 2007, 4.

16. Ibid., 12-14.

17. Lewis, M.A. et al. "Drugs, Poverty, Pregnancy and Foster Care in Los Angeles, California, 1989-1991." *The Western Journal of Medicine* 163, 1995, 435-440.

18. Ibid.

19. Centers for Disease Control and Prevention, 2008.

20. Wulczyn, F. and K.B. Hislop. "Babies in Foster Care: The Numbers Call for Attention." *Zero to Three Journal*, April/May 2002, 14.

21. U.S. Department of Health and Human Services, Administration for Children and Families. *The AFCARS Report*. Washington, D.C.: Administration on Children, Youth and Families, Children's Bureau, 2006. Available at www.acf.hhs.gov/programs/cb.

22. Ibid.

23. Kemp, S.P. and J.M. Bodonyi. "Infants Who Stay in Foster Care: Child Characteristics and Permanency Outcomes of Legally Free Children First Placed as Infants." *Child and Family Social Work* 5, 2000, 101.

24. Wulczyn, F. "Status at Birth and Infant Foster Care Placement in New York City." In *Child Welfare Research Review* 1. Edited by R. Barth, J.D. Berrick and N. Gilbert. New York City: Columbia University Press, 1994, 146-184.

25. Wulczyn and Hislop, 2002, 14.

26. Wulczyn et al, 2002, 466-468.

27. Ibid.

28. Kemp and Bodonyi, 2000, 102-104.

29. Jones Harden, B. *Infants in the Child Welfare System: A Developmental Framework for Policy and Practice*. Washington, DC: Zero to Three, 2007, 56-57.

30. Wulczyn, F. and K.B. Hislop. *The Placement of Infants in Foster Care*. Chicago: Chapin Hall Center for Children, University of Chicago, 2000.

31. Ibid.

32. Kemp and Bodonyi, 2000, 99; Wulczyn et al., 2002, 466.

33. *RESOURCE GUIDELINES: Improving Court Practice in Abuse and Neglect Cases*. Reno, NV: National Council of Juvenile and Family Court Judges, 1995.

Promoting Physical Health

Promoting Physical Health

Initial Health Information Gathering

▶ Ensure detailed health histories are obtained from the birth parents and other caregivers at placement.

▶ Ensure medical information is obtained when a newborn enters care from the hospital.

▶ Ensure the child receives an initial health screen within 24 hours of entering care.

▶ Ask the child welfare agency to report health screen results at the initial hearing and ensure the child welfare agency is keeping all of a child's medical records on file.

▶ Request additional health assessments to address missing information.

Comprehensive Physical Assessment

▶ Require a comprehensive health assessment within 30 days of placement.

▶ Ensure necessary health care records and consents are available.

▶ Ensure the comprehensive assessment includes developmental and mental health screens by a qualified provider.

▶ Request assessment results and ensure services are in place.

Immunizations

▶ Ensure the child has been properly immunized.

  ▶ Ask about immunization at the first hearing.

  ▶ Ensure immunizations are complete and up-to-date for the child's age.

  ▶ Require catchup immunizations if necessary.

Routine Medical Screening

▶ Ensure the child has received all appropriate screenings.

chapter 2

Coordinated Medical Care

▶ Require a medical home.

▶ Address barriers to using a medical home.

    ▶ Make placement decisions with continuity of health care in mind.

    ▶ Ensure the initial placement for a child in care is carefully selected and work to maintain the integrity of this placement.

    ▶ If a change is needed, try to keep the child in the same geographic area and make sure caseworkers and foster parents understand the importance of the medical home.

▶ Ask if the child has a health passport.

Oral Health

▶ Ensure the child receives appropriate dental services.

▶ Help each child access a dental home.

▶ Remove barriers to dental care.

Barriers to Health Care Access

▶ Find out if the child has health insurance.

▶ Identify other barriers to the child's access to medical services.

Many infants and young children enter foster care with complex physical health needs. Acute illnesses, diseases, infections and compromised bodily organs or systems often result from the child's maltreatment and inadequate health care. As the judge, you can affect these young lives when they are most vulnerable and when services and supports can have the greatest impact.

Becoming familiar with the physical health needs and characteristics of each child in your court can help you make the best decisions for these children and their families. You play a key role by:

- ensuring information about the child's physical health is gathered at the start of the case;
- requesting a comprehensive medical assessment to identify gaps in knowledge about the child's physical health;
- asking specific questions about the child's physical health and medical needs (including whether she has a medical home or regular source of routine medical care);
- ensuring birth parents and foster caregivers receive education and training to meet the child's special health needs; and
- securing medical services and supports to treat the child's physical health issues.

Initial Health Information Gathering

When a very young child enters foster care, an opportunity exists to identify and address any unmet physical health needs. Seeking health information as early as possible after placement helps ensure that immediate and long-term health needs of young children are met. To get a complete picture of a young child's physical health upon entering care, take the following steps.

Ensure detailed health histories are obtained from the birth parents and other caregivers at placement.

The child's health history before entering care lays the foundation for services she will receive while in care, so it is essential to obtain this information as soon as possible. As time passes, it may become harder to secure this information. Encourage the agency to follow the American Academy of Pediatrics' (AAP) recommendations by gathering critical information when removing the child, including:

- where the child has been receiving health care;
- immunization record or history;
- any chronic medical conditions (e.g., asthma, sickle cell disease, epilepsy);
- past surgeries or past hospitalizations;

- medications the child takes;
- medical equipment the child uses (e.g., glasses, hearing aids, nebulizers, wheelchairs, epipens);
- any allergies;
- the child's birthplace (so birth records can be obtained);[1] and
- a family health history (particularly hereditable or communicable diseases).

Any additional medical or immunization records in the home, as well as medications and medical equipment, should also be obtained when the child is removed. Agency staff should ensure that the medical records travel with the child. Caseworkers can obtain a more complete health history by using a comprehensive health history form to interview parents. The AAP is developing one and will post it on its Healthy Foster Care America Web site (www.aap.org/advocacy/HFCA/). Daycare providers, grandparents, and others who regularly care for the child can also be rich sources of information.

Ensure medical information is obtained when a newborn enters care from the hospital.

Many infants are placed into care directly from the hospital.[2] When newborns enter care from the hospital, it is important for the agency or caregiver to obtain from the hospital staff:

- instructions for immediate care (e.g., treatment for existing health conditions, signs and symptoms requiring urgent health care);
- information about where the infant will receive follow-up care— primary care and referrals to specialists, if any;
- results of any state-mandated screenings to identify conditions for which the infant will need follow-up care (e.g., genetic defects, metabolic problems);
- a list of immunizations given at the hospital;
- results of the newborn hearing screen;
- any information about risks to later healthy development, such as prematurity, low birth weight, prenatal substance exposures, and lack of prenatal care;[3] and
- birth records and the hospital discharge summary.

Ensure the child receives an initial health screen within 24 hours of entering care.[4]

This initial evaluation:

- screens for acute illnesses;

- identifies chronic diseases;
- documents signs of abuse, neglect, or infectious diseases; and
- assesses any hygiene or nutritional concerns.

These preliminary observations should inform the placement decision and follow-up for health problems. Ask whether the initial health screen identified lower than expected height, weight, or head circumference measurements or obesity. If so, order further evaluation since these findings may suggest growth delays, poor nutrition, or poor general health. (See sidebar, page 46, for an in-depth discussion of failure to thrive.) Having baseline measures of the child's health can help detect disruptions in growth over time. The health screen also allows the clinician to share age-appropriate strategies to help caregivers support children who are experiencing acute grief associated with removal.

An initial health screen can help detect significant physical, mental health, and developmental problems of children when they enter foster care. Initial placement provides a chance to identify, treat and refer infants and young children with unmet needs. Because children placed in care may return home within 30 days, an initial health screen should be conducted promptly to identify any significant medical needs. Failure to identify these needs places the child at risk for poor health outcomes. It also affects placement adjustment, as potentially serious behavioral, developmental, and physical health problems compromise placement stability and may impact permanency options.

Ask the child welfare agency to report health screen results at the initial hearing and ensure the child welfare agency is keeping all of a child's medical records on file.

Caseworkers should come to court ready to summarize and discuss the results of a child's health assessment. If a child has not yet been assessed, or the results are not yet available, find out why. Ask the caseworker to obtain the information and file a supplemental report. Set clear expectations for agency caseworkers and attorneys for what health information you expect every time they are in your courtroom.

Request additional health assessments to address missing information.

If the health screening report was incomplete, or indicated a need for urgent follow-up, evaluation, or care, require the caseworker to address those gaps and file a supplemental report within a set period.

Comprehensive Physical Assessment

Require a comprehensive health assessment within 30 days of placement.

The AAP recommends that all children undergo a comprehensive health assessment within 30 days of placement in care.[5] Children who lacked routine health care before entering the child welfare system are vulnerable to medical, mental health, and developmental conditions that are normally detected during routine health evaluations.

As part of a comprehensive health assessment, a health care provider gathers information to learn about risks for ongoing health problems. These include:

- chronic conditions
- hospitalizations
- past surgeries
- medications
- allergies
- immunizations
- behaviors and emotional health
- developmental skills
- adjustment to foster care and visitation[6]

The child's prenatal and birth histories are critical as the health provider needs to know about circumstances such as:

- substance exposure during pregnancy
- birth weight
- problems at delivery
- infectious risks for the child
- family health problems that could affect the child
- newborn screening results

This information helps medical providers make care decisions, including recommendations about treatment, referrals, and follow-up, and also helps judges, lawyers, and caseworkers plan for placement and permanency. In addition, the clinician can provide caregivers problem-specific health information, child care recommendations, and strategies to promote the child's emotional and behavioral health.

Ensure necessary health care records and consents are available.

The child welfare agency must provide all relevant records so the health professional can conduct a complete health assessment. These include all past and current records from primary and specialty care providers, hospital records, and agency records containing relevant medical, social, and family health information. Additionally, each state has requirements for obtaining consent to health care of children in the child welfare system. Become familiar with your state's requirements so you can ensure that proper consents for routine and emergency care are secured and a child's care is not delayed. This includes ensuring that birth parents cooperate in signing consents, providing health histories, and attending health visits, when appropriate.

Ensure the comprehensive assessment includes developmental and mental health screens by a qualified provider.

A comprehensive health assessment includes several screenings for problems common to children in the child welfare system, including developmental delays and some mental health concerns. Ensure that these initial screens have occurred for children in your courtroom. (See Chapter 3 for more information, including early intervention services under Part C of the Individuals with Disabilities Education Act.)

Request assessment results and ensure services are in place.

At early hearings, ask the agency if a comprehensive health assessment has occurred (or is planned). Require a summary of the results be given in court or submitted within one week after the assessment occurs. Ask the agency to provide any missing information in a supplemental report to the court before the next scheduled hearing. Any necessary services should begin before the next scheduled hearing if they are not already in place.

As the case continues, ensure that parents have had regular contact with health professionals (medical, mental health, developmental, and dental) and understand their child's care before approving unsupervised visits, and certainly before approving overnight visits or permitting the child to return home.

Children in foster care with communication delays and problems with personal-social and cognitive development should also be screened for autism, as discussed in Chapter 3.

Immunizations

Ensure the child has been properly immunized.

Immunizations protect children against potentially devastating diseases, and are critical for children who have received inadequate health care. Proper immunization decreases a child's susceptibility to many illnesses, some of which have potential long-term effects. Incomplete immunization also generally means a child lacks medical care from a regular provider. An unimmunized child should be considered at risk for many medical problems.

Ask about immunization at the first hearing.

At the initial hearing, ask if a child's immunization records are available and if the child is up-to-date for recommended immunizations. If the child is missing immunizations, require the agency to work with the child's health provider to obtain missing information or provide needed immunizations. Also ask about the immunization status of caregivers. For conditions the child cannot be immunized against because of age or health status, it may be especially important that caregivers are immunized.

Ensure immunizations are complete and up-to-date for the child's age.

All children new to foster care should have a health screen followed by a comprehensive medical evaluation. To achieve this goal, be sure to ask the caseworker to collaborate with health providers to obtain immunization records or begin "immunization catchup" for children at the time of the comprehensive health screen.

Order that the child receive immunizations consistent with the most recent nationally recommended immunization guidelines published jointly by the Centers for Disease Control and Prevention (CDC), the Advisory Committee on Immunization Practices (ACIP), and the AAP, available at www.cdc.gov/vaccines/recs/acip/. Federal law requires that state Medicaid programs use these guidelines, so payment should not be an issue for most children.[7]

Require catchup immunizations if necessary.

Allow about 30 days for caseworkers and health providers to investigate immunization history by exploring avenues such as old health records, immunization registries, and school and child care records. This avoids repeating immunizations the child has already had. Also require that doctors treating children in foster care use the national immunization information system (www.cdc.gov/vaccines/programs/iis/default.htm) to ensure children are not overimmunized. If any necessary immunizations have not been given, order catchup immunizations according to CDC, ACIP and AAP combined guidelines, beginning at or shortly after the comprehensive health assessment.

Children entering foster care as unaccompanied refugee minors may have inaccurate and incomplete immunization records and may need blood tests before beginning catchup immunizations. Their health screenings should address health risks specific to their countries of origin. Children with immune problems (e.g., due to chemotherapy, treatment with steroids, or HIV infection), should not receive live virus vaccines, so it is essential that health care providers have complete information on the child's health status before administering these vaccines.

Routine Medical Screening

Ensure the child has received all appropriate screenings.

Catching problems and starting services early gives children a better chance of healing or achieving optimal control of health problems. Fortunately, most children in foster care are Medicaid eligible, and therefore eligible for Medicaid's Early and Periodic Screening, Diagnosis, and Treatment (EPSDT) program. The EPSDT program provides essential preventive health services to at-risk children. As part of a comprehensive health assessment, children are eligible for a variety of screening procedures, including evaluation for:

- hearing and vision problems
- lead exposure
- communicable diseases
- nutrition status
- anemia
- growth problems
- mental health issues
- medical problems

For any problems identified by screenings or assessments, order that birth parents and foster caregivers receive assistance to properly care for the child (e.g., training on how to use a nebulizer, education about managing diabetes).

Hearing, speech and language

Ask the agency if the child received a hearing screen at birth and regular speech, language, and hearing screenings thereafter. If not, require that they be done before the next court date. Also ask if any reports from parents or caregivers raise hearing or language concerns. If so, require an assessment and any indicated services.

Normal hearing is essential to a young child's speech and language acquisition, adjustment, and emotional development. Failure to detect hearing loss hampers development in these areas and can impair later learning and academic achievement. Detecting hearing loss and intervening within the first six months of life helps prevent or reduce these outcomes.[8] Annual hearing screening should be conducted for any child with a family history of hearing impairment, and those with syndromes that place the child at risk for hearing impairment (e.g., Down syndrome, Usher syndrome, Treacher Collins syndrome).

Hearing loss can result from congenital diseases, infections such as ear infections and meningitis, head injury, neglect of health problems, or use of medications that damage hearing.[9] In addition, a number of factors put children at risk for developing a hearing problem later in life, including structural abnormalities of the ear or face, certain exposures in the newborn or late gestational period, and speech and language delays.

All states but one provide hearing evaluations for newborns.[10] These screens detect most hearing loss due to congenital problems. Many children referred for follow-up hearing exams after the initial screen never go back for those evaluations, however, so it is important to ask if necessary follow-up has occurred.[11] The AAP also recommends a formal objective hearing screen at four years of age in addition to screenings for all newborns.[12]

Speech and language disorders may occur from hearing loss, early neglect and deprivation, or a variety of genetic or medical conditions. Speech disorders may include problems with how speech sounds are pronounced (articulation), the rhythm of speech (fluency or stuttering), the quality of voice or some combination of problems.[13] Language disorders stem from a problem understanding and/or using spoken or written words or sign language.[14] Swallowing disorders, feeding problems, or cognitive impairments may also signal speech-language issues.

A child's speech and language development follows a predictable pattern throughout the first five years of life, beginning at age two months. During the first 18 months, children should be able to imitate sounds, form simple words, point, and use two-word phrases.[15] An important sign of normal social and language development is a child's ability to expand their use of language to convey thoughts and feelings and to show increasing comprehension of the world around them through such actions as pointing, gesturing, or responding to simple commands.[16]

Older children, through age two, should begin to use two-to-three word phrases and understand questions. Children aged two to three years should be able to form short sentences (four to five words or more) and tell brief stories.[17] As children get older and their speech and language develops, their words become more intelligible to adults who do not regularly spend time with them; for three

Speech, Language, and Hearing Milestones for Young Children

	Hearing and Understanding	**Talking and Communicating**
Birth–6 months	Startle to loud sounds. Respond to changes in tone of your voice.	Cry differently for different needs. Babbling sounds more speech-like with many different sounds, including p, b and m.
7–12 months	Enjoy games like peek-a-boo and pat-a-cake. Recognize words for common items like "cup," "shoe," "book," or "juice."	Imitate different speech sounds. Use gestures to communicate (waving, holding arms to be picked up).
12–24 months	Follow simple directions and understand simple questions ("Roll the ball," "Kiss the baby," "Where's your shoe?"). Point to pictures in a book when named.	Say more words every month. Put two words together ("more cookie," "no juice," "mommy book").
24–36 months (2–3 years)	Understand differences in meaning ("go-stop," "in-on," "big-little," "up-down"). Follow two requests ("Get the book and put it on the table.").	Use two or three words to talk about and ask for things. Speech is understood by familiar listeners most of the time.
36–48 months (3–4 years)	Hear you when you call from another room. Answer simple who, what, where, and why questions.	People outside of the family usually understand child's speech. Use a lot of sentences that have four or more words.
48–60 months (4–5 years)	Pay attention to a short story and answer simple questions about it. Hear and understand most of what is said at home and in school.	Communicate easily with other children and adults. Use sentences that give lots of details (e.g., "The biggest peach is mine.").

Source: Adapted from American Speech-Language-Hearing Association. *How Does Your Child Hear and Talk?* Available at www.asha.org/public/speech/development/chart.htm (last accessed February 18, 2009). View the online chart for a complete list of milestones and ways to help children who are not reaching them.

year olds, 75% to 80% intelligible speech is a good guideline.[18] Children aged three to four should have a vocabulary of over 1,000 words and should ask "why" and "how" questions.[19] The American Speech-Language-Hearing Association lists more hearing, understanding, and talking milestones for different age ranges at www.asha.org/public/speech/development/chart.htm. The absence of certain behaviors (pointing and showing, eye contact with caregiver, limited speech) merits screening for autistic spectrum disorder (see Chapter 3) or other speech-language and developmental problems.

Very young children may also be evaluated for hearing problems when adults observe hearing difficulties, inattention, or erratic responses to sound. Most hearing deficits are uncovered when a parent has concerns and requests an assessment. Parents often identify hearing problems up to a year before a physician would,[20] and can also be essential in catching speech and language delays. Since children in foster care often lack a consistent caregiver who can detect subtle abnormalities or delays, they may be less likely to be identified early. Children in care should undergo regular screenings for deficits in hearing, speech, and language development to ensure their healthy development. Whenever *any* caregiver suspects hearing, speech, or language problems, a formal evaluation should occur.

Vision

Ask if the child's eye exam was abnormal *as a newborn* and at *later checkups*. For children older than three, ask if a vision screen has been completed. (Until age four, children may not cooperate in identifying shapes reliably, so they are not ready for vision screens. They can still receive eye exams that check for expected reflexes, responses to light, and range of eye movements.) If not, require a vision screen before the next hearing. Require the agency to report the results of vision screenings, and to start any recommended services. If a child has impaired vision, ensure he has current prescription glasses.

Vision problems are the fourth most common disability for children in the United States,[21] and are more prevalent among children in foster care. Screening for vision problems detects conditions that can result in serious visual impairment, including blindness. It also detects other diseases that can affect the body.[22] Undetected vision problems can lead to poor school performance and can be life threatening if they lead to a more serious disease.

The AAP recommends all children have a vision exam as newborns and at all routine health visits. A formal vision screen should be attempted at age three (if the child is uncooperative, a repeat screen should be attempted in six months).[23] If screening is unsuccessful despite repeated attempts, the child should be referred (by age four years) to an ophthalmologist trained in examining children.[24]

Screening and Placement Can Decrease Lead Levels

A study[1] of children in foster care, their siblings, and the general population found:

▶ before entering foster care, children were twice as likely as other children to have elevated blood lead levels; and

▶ after placement, the children were less than half as likely to have high lead levels.

Practice Tips:

▶ **Ensure children receiving services in their own home or in kinship care**, as well as children entering care, are screened for lead exposure.

▶ **Consider environmental and behavioral factors** that may lead to increased lead exposure when making placement decisions. Of particular concern are houses built prior to 1979, especially if they have peeling paint, and children who have the eating disorder pica (which involves regularly ingesting nonfood items).

Source:
1. Chung, E., Webb, D. et al. "A Comparison of Elevated Blood Lead Levels Among Children Living in Foster Care, Their Siblings, and the General Population." *Pediatrics* 107(5), 2001, e81-85.

Lead exposure

Ask if the child had a lead screening at *nine to twelve months* of age and *annually thereafter*. If not, require a screening for lead exposure by a pediatric health professional as soon as possible. If the screening reveals an issue, order an investigation into the source of the lead.

A prior history of abuse and neglect, developmental delay, behavior problems, failure to thrive, and poverty are all associated with an increased risk for lead exposure and poisoning.[25] Children living in poverty are at high risk for lead poisoning, but only 20-30% of this group is screened for exposure. Because most children entering foster care have many of these risk factors, including poverty, they should be considered at high risk for lead exposure.

Lead poisoning harms a child's health and development, and can lead to impaired learning, lower academic achievement and intelligence, abnormal behavioral development, decreased growth and hearing, and damage to the brain, kidney, and blood-forming process. For children in foster care, the AAP recommends blood lead screening at nine to twelve months of age, with yearly screenings through age six.[26] For children with elevated lead levels, the pediatric health professional should follow the CDC guidelines for more frequent screening and/or treatment.[27]

If the child's current home (or the home the child is expected to move to when case plan goals are reached) has dangerous lead levels, the court should order that lead hazards be reduced to safe levels through abatement or other methods. Some jurisdictions have federal Department of Housing and Urban Development funding to reduce lead hazards, but if your jurisdiction does not (or there are long waiting lists), order the agency to pay for the work (or help the family find new housing) as part of their required reasonable efforts.

Communicable diseases

- **Sexually transmitted infections:** Many young children in foster care have birth parents whose sexual histories are unknown and who struggle with substance abuse. These exposures place children entering care at high risk for infection with HIV, hepatitis B, hepatitis C, syphilis, and congenital herpes. Children with a history of sexual abuse are also at risk for other sexually transmitted diseases.[28] Ask if the child has been screened for *HSV (herpes), syphilis, hepatitis B, and hepatitis C.*

- **HIV:** A risk assessment for HIV exposure should be conducted,[29] and, if positive, the child should have a blood test to screen for HIV infection once consent is obtained (states vary on who may give consent for testing children in care and the procedures for obtaining consent). Some states' newborn screens also include an HIV test. Order any necessary screenings before the next hearing, and ask the agency to file a supplemental report with the screening results. Early screening and treatment for these conditions promotes the long-term healthy development of children in foster care.

  For young children, detecting HIV is also critical to ensuring an infected child receives modified immunizations to maximize the protective effect of vaccination, while avoiding harm.[30]

- **Tuberculosis:** Tuberculosis (TB) exposure is more common among certain groups, and occurs through exposure to the respiratory droplets of an infected person (e.g., droplets expelled through a cough or sneeze). Those who are or have been incarcerated, live in crowded conditions, or immigrate from certain countries are at high risk. Testing for TB exposure is recommended for all children placed in foster care beginning at 12 months of age. Children should be re-screened every three-to-five years while in foster care or whenever an exposure is suspected. A positive

Data Supports HIV Testing for Infants and Young Children

Children in foster care at all ages are at increased risk for HIV infection. Studies have shown:

▶ Inner-city newborns placed directly in foster care were eight times more likely to be born to an HIV-positive mother than other newborns.[1]

▶ Health care providers did not detect infection in 17.7% of HIV-infected children studied until four years of age.[2]

▶ 36 out of 42 children who acquired HIV during the perinatal period did not display symptoms of infection until after age four.[3]

Practice Tips:

▶ **Assess HIV status of all children in foster care** since symptoms are not always apparent. Some risk factors include maternal substance abuse, multiple sexual partners, unprotected sex, the presence of other vertically transmitted infections, and sexual abuse. For children who enter foster care secondary to sexual abuse, HIV testing should be done at the time of the incident, and then at six weeks, three months, and six months after the incident.[4]

▶ **Obtain consent for HIV screening.** If the mother's HIV status was not determined during pregnancy, the HIV exposure status of the newborn or infant should be determined. The AAP recommends discussing testing the newborn with the mother after birth to obtain consent. If the mother refuses consent, or if the authority to consent for medical care has been transferred to the foster care agency, the agency or the court should give consent.[5]

▶ **Older children, including toddlers and preschoolers, should also be assessed.** The factors that led to foster care placement often correlate with increased risk for HIV infection. Children may display no or only mild symptoms of infection for several years.

▶ **Know the risk factors.** Understand the risk for HIV infection in infants and other young children in foster care and order necessary evaluations when risk factors are present.

Sources:

1. Nicholas, S., et al. "Maternal Newborn Human Immunodeficiency Virus Infection in Harlem." *Archives of Pediatric and Adolescent Medicine* 148, 1994, 813-819.

2. Persaud D. et al. "Delayed Recognition of Human Immunodeficiency Virus Infection in Preadolescent Children." *Pediatrics* 90, 1992, 688-691 (study not specific to children in foster care).

3. Grubman S. et al. "Older Children and Adolescents with Perinatally Acquired Human Immunodeficiency Virus Infection." *Pediatrics* 95, 1995, 657-663 (study not specific to children in foster care).

4. American Academy of Pediatrics, Task Force on Health Care for Children. *Fostering Health: Health Care for Children and Adolescents in Foster Care*, 2005.

5. American Academy of Pediatrics Committee on Pediatric AIDS. *Identification and Care of HIV-Exposed and HIV-Infected Infants, Children and Adolescents in Foster Care*, 2000.

TB screening test requires evaluation by a specialist in TB (local health departments can identify these specialists).

- **Parasitic diseases:** The small population of refugee minors in foster care often come from countries in which parasitic disease is prevalent. Refugees from certain areas of the world, such as Africa and Southeast Asia, should be screened for parasitic disease and treated according to AAP Redbook or CDC guidelines.

Malnutrition

Malnourished children may not meet recommended growth parameters (weight, length, and head circumference) or may have hair, skin, teeth, or mouth abnormalities.[31] Any of these findings on a screening exam should prompt questions about the child's nutritional health.

The special dietary needs of infants and young children (who cannot eat most "adult" foods and instead require formula, baby cereal, and other foods high in vitamins, minerals, and protein) can be costly and difficult for some foster caregivers to maintain. Infants and children up to their fifth birthday may be eligible for nutrition assistance services under the Special Supplemental Nutrition Program for Women, Infants and Children (WIC).[32] WIC benefits include supplemental nutritious foods, nutrition education and counseling at WIC clinics, and screening and referral to other services.

To ensure the nutritional needs of infants and children in care are met, ask whether their nutrition status has been evaluated and whether their growth parameters are normal for their age. Also ask whether a child is being fed an age-appropriate diet as this shows a caregiver's awareness of and attention to a child's needs. For example, children less than one year should not receive regular milk and children less than two should receive a diet with adequate calories and fat for brain development. Consider barriers to food access that may contribute to suboptimal dietary practices. Require the agency to refer caregivers to resources that provide nutritious options for children in their care (e.g., WIC and its "Farmers Market Nutrition Program"). Be sensitive to the fact that dietary choices may be influenced by cultural beliefs and practices.

Many children in foster care have feeding difficulties. Some were premature infants with medical complications that delayed the start of oral feeding. Others have developmental delays, sensory problems or behavioral issues that interfere with feeding. Food insecurity before foster care may lead to behaviors such as hoarding of food, gorging, eating spoiled or discarded food, pica, or strong but unhealthy food preferences.

How the Court Can Support Breastfeeding

Infants who are breastfed have 21% lower mortality rates, and may be less likely to develop diabetes, asthma, leukemia, obesity and other diseases later in life.[1] Breastfeeding also protects against or minimizes the severity of many infectious diseases including bacterial meningitis, respiratory tract infections, and ear infections.[2]

Practice Tips:

▶ **Order daily visitation** to support breastfeeding when safety is not an issue.

▶ **Ensure the mother has the equipment she needs** to preserve milk for her child when they are not together (e.g., a breast pump).

▶ **Order a consultation with a pediatric or obstetric health professional** if a mother's medical condition or other life circumstance raises questions about the appropriateness of breastfeeding. Although breastfeeding may not be in the child's best interest in some situations (e.g., the mother is abusing drugs, has HIV, or is receiving chemotherapy), breastfeeding is the healthiest choice for most infants.[3]

▶ **Ensure the agency knows about local resources** to support breastfeeding, and has educated the mother on this topic. (La Leche League International maintains a list of resources in each state at www.llli.org/WebUS.html.)

Source:

1. American Academy of Pediatrics, Section on Breastfeeding. "Breastfeeding and the Use of Human Milk." *Pediatrics* 115(2), 2005, 496-506.

2. Ibid.

3. Ibid.

The other form of malnutrition is obesity, which is now more prevalent in children new to foster care than failure to thrive or growth failure. Almost all obesity results from consuming too many calories, lack of activity, and inadequate nutrients in the diet. This problem is compounded when foster parents have difficulty "limiting" access to food in the foster home because it upsets the child or they fear being accused of neglect.

During the first year, regular feeding helps the child trust that his needs will be met. This promotes healthy attachment to caregivers, which is important for healthy emotional and mental development (see Chapter 3). Older children should have a diet rich in vegetables, fruits, whole grains, low fat dairy foods, and protein sources. Desserts, unhealthy snacks, and processed foods should be minimized. Meals should occur at predictable times, at the table, in a pleasant context that engages family members. Portions should be appropriate to the child's age.

Children with Chronic Health Care Needs Benefit from Specialized Nutrition Services

Compared to other children from the same socioeconomic background, children in foster care have much higher rates of chronic physical disabilities.[1] Children with such special health care needs experience greater rates of nutrition-related health problems because their chronic condition may alter their appetite or food intake.[2] Environmental factors may also affect access to or acceptance of food. [3]

Nutrition-related special health needs may include:

▸ delayed growth

▸ difficulty feeding and eliminating

▸ interactions between foods and medications

▸ altered appetites

▸ unusual eating habits

▸ early childhood dental problems

▸ difficulty maintaining a healthy weight (either overweight or underweight)

Practice Tips:

When chronic illness and nutrition concerns arise:

▸ **Ask whether the child's nutrition status has been assessed.** If not, order an assessment.

▸ **Order an assessment for early intervention services.** Early intervention services provide access to dietitians, occupational therapists, physical therapists, and speech and language pathologists who are trained to address nutrition and feeding issues.

Sources:

1. American Academy of Pediatrics, Committee on Early Childhood, Adoption and Dependent Care. "Health Care of Young Children in Foster Care." *Pediatrics* 109(3), March 2002, 536-541.

2. Hagan J.F., J.S. Shaw and P.M. Duncan, eds. *Bright Futures: Guidelines for Health Supervision of Infants, Children, and Adolescents*, 3d ed. Elk Grove Village, IL: American Academy of Pediatrics, 2008.

3. Ibid.

Coordinated Medical Care

The average stay in foster care is roughly 28 months,[33] and approximately two-thirds of children in care for 24 months or longer have three or more different placements while in care.[34] For this reason, children in foster care are less likely to receive ongoing care by the same provider than other children. Having contact with a single health care provider is crucial for children who are slowly adjusting to separating from a primary caregiver and adapting to a new placement.

Preventive Health Care Schedule

Age	Recommended Frequency of Visits
Birth to six months	Monthly
Six months to one year	Every two months
One to two years	Every three months
Two years through adolescence	Every six months

In addition to age-based visits, AAP also recommends supplemental visits at critical child welfare junctures, including:

▶ system entry;

▶ placement transitions;

▶ significant changes within the home environment (health issues or death of a caregiver, disruption of sibling from a home, etc.);

▶ when significant issues arise around visitation;

▶ when any concern is raised regarding potential child abuse or neglect;

▶ deterioration in child behavior or developmental skills;

▶ deterioration in health; and

▶ system exit—either based on discharge, termination of parental rights, or adoption.

Source: American Academy of Pediatrics, Committee on Early Childhood, Adoption and Dependent Care. "Health Care of Young Children in Foster Care." *Pediatrics* 109(3), March 2002, 539 (supplemental examples provided by Moira Szilagyi, MD, PhD, FAAP, Vice-chair of the AAPs Task Force on Foster Care).

Ideally that health provider is familiar with the impact of complex trauma, separation, and loss on the emotional and developmental health of children in foster care. Since the harmful experiences of children in care can negatively impact their health and well-being, the AAP recommends an enhanced preventive health care schedule for these children. Regular contact with a knowledgeable medical home provider (discussed below) helps detect subtle changes in the child over time, and supports and educates foster parents, who are the primary therapeutic intervention for the child in care. The AAP recommends an increased preventive health care schedule for children in foster care (see above).

To help ensure adequate health care:

• Ask at each hearing when the child's last medical appointment was, and when the next one is scheduled.

• Require that additional appointments be scheduled at critical points in the child's case or according to the AAP age-based recommendations above.

- Ask the caseworker to obtain a health update after each well-child visit and to incorporate that information into the permanency plan in a meaningful way (e.g., for the child with asthma, all current and potential caregivers should have asthma education and understand the signs and symptoms, which medications the child needs, how and when to administer them, and when to seek help).
- Ensure all current and potential caregivers know the child's doctor's name and number.

Require a medical home.

Ask if the child has a medical home, a single source of coordinated health care and if the caseworker receives health updates from that resource. A medical home ensures a child is being seen frequently (because records will accurately show the last visit) and allows health care providers to develop a relationship with the child.

A "medical home" offers coordinated, comprehensive, compassionate health care that is continuous over time. Continuity of care in the medical home promotes better outcomes for children, including increased immunization rates, fewer emergency department visits, decreased hospitalization, and improved perceptions of quality of care. This continuity can be especially important to children in care, who have greater health and social needs. The medical home may be essential to timely identify health care needs and deliver appropriate health services for children in foster care.

Other advantages of the foster care medical home are it maintains a detailed health record for the child in foster care, develops care plans for children with special health care needs, assumes responsibility for care coordination, and exchanges health information with child welfare at regular intervals. Recognizing this, the AAP stresses that children in foster care should receive continuity of care through a medical home.[35]

A medical home is centrally located, accessible, and accepts a variety of insurance. It is family-centered and offers culturally effective care. One practitioner acts as a single point of contact for a child and knows the needs of children in the foster care system. The practitioner oversees primary care and periodic reassessments of the physical, developmental, and emotional health of the children under her care.[36] The primary care practitioner for the child in foster care can facilitate access to all other mental health, developmental, and dental health care services, and maintain uninterrupted treatment and health information for the child.

Another benefit of a medical home is its cost-effectiveness. Children who use emergency departments, walk-in clinics, or urgent care facilities for regular medical care receive services that cost more and are less effective, particularly for children with special health care needs.[37]

A medical home can also reduce the duration of inpatient hospitalization and medical errors, because the child's provider knows her health history. Care by a skilled pediatric health professional in the context of a medical home helps the courts and child welfare agencies' efforts to support caregivers, improve health outcomes, create stable placements, and promote permanency for children.

Address barriers to using a medical home.

For the system's most medically needy children, meeting the medical home recommendation will be difficult. Finding health providers familiar with the impact of complex trauma on children and families, willing to accept Medicaid and to spend the extra time for the poor reimbursement Medicaid offers, is a challenge. Maintaining continuity of care with a single provider for children experiencing multiple placements or moving into and out of foster care is difficult. To address these concerns and support medical home use, take the following steps:

- **Make placement decisions with continuity of health care in mind.** Reducing multiple placements for children in foster care promotes medical home use, which reduces placement instability.

- **Ensure the initial placement for a child in care is carefully selected** and work to maintain the integrity of this placement. For children with complex health care needs, a medical home provider who knows the foster care agency and foster parents in the area can help select placements for children.

- **If a change is needed, try to keep the child in the same geographic area** and make sure caseworkers and foster parents understand the importance of the medical home. This also promotes educational stability and maintains the child's other connections within the community.

Ask if the child has a health passport.

Continuity of health care services is particularly challenging for children in foster care whose placements change frequently. Besides establishing medical homes, health data-sharing efforts can help ensure continuity of services. Several states have developed a health passport for children in foster care. Health passports are snapshots of a child's health history that provide useful information to the child's health providers, caseworkers, and caregivers and help ensure appropriate health care is received while minimizing medical errors and duplicated services. The health passport may be in electronic or paper format, or a combination, and

Health Disparities and Culturally Effective Health Care

Black infants have more than twice the infant mortality rate of White infants, and are almost twice as likely to have low birth weights.[1] Black children are also more likely than White children to have asthma, to be hospitalized for asthma, and to die from asthma.[2] They are also more likely to be uninsured, have elevated lead levels in their blood, be overweight, and be diagnosed with type-2 diabetes.[3]

In response to these disparities and other factors, the AAP believes all children should receive culturally effective pediatric care.[4] It encourages increased training for health professionals on cultural diversity, and increased institutional efforts and government funding to support culturally effective care.[5]

Practice Tips:

▶ **Be aware of cultural and racial differences in your communities** that may be affecting health service delivery and use.

▶ **Learn about health disparities or cultural attitudes towards health** common among people in your jurisdiction.

▶ **Partner with local medical organizations to address health disparities** (e.g., by serving on a task force addressing the issue, or testifying on the issue, along with medical professionals, to local or state government).

Sources:

1. Disparities in Children's Health and Health Coverage, Children's Defense Fund Healthy Child Campaign. Available at www.childrensdefense.org/child-research-data-publications/data/childrens-health-disparities-factsheet.pdf.

2. Ibid.

3. Ibid.

4. American Academy of Pediatrics Committee on Pediatric Workforce. "Ensuring Culturally Effective Pediatric Care: Implications for Education and Health Policy." *Pediatrics* 114(6), 2004, 1677-1685.

5. Ibid.

summarizes essential health information including medical problems, allergies, chronic medications, and immunization data, as well as social service and family history. The passport can also be used to record behavioral health, dental, hearing, and vision services.

The passport is available to all of the child's health providers, regardless of placement changes. Paper passports alone are less successful because they get lost or forgotten or are not filled out. Some states have better success with Web-based secure health passports which maintain data on a specific child from multiple data systems and can include immunization, EPSDT, lead, WIC, and other data. However, there are often no requirements or incentives for providers to fill them out and passports are only useful if updated regularly. Health passports are more useful where medical homes dedicated to the care of the child in foster care do not exist.

Encourage agencies to use health passports and ensure the foster parent has access to a health passport when the child is first placed. Instruct the foster parent to bring the record to all health evaluations, and make sure the record goes with the child if placement changes. When electronic records are available, ensure confidentiality protections are applied.

Oral Health

Ensure the child receives appropriate dental services.

Early childhood caries (previously known as baby bottle tooth decay) is a common infectious disease among children, according to a U.S. Surgeon General's report, more common even than asthma or hay fever. Although this disease is chronic, transmissible and *progressive*, it can also be prevented, and is manageable once acquired. It affects infants from all racial and socioeconomic backgrounds, but low-income children are especially at risk.[38] More than 40 percent of children show signs of tooth decay before reaching kindergarten.[39] Tooth decay and cavities cause pain and potentially life-threatening swelling. They also affect learning, communication, behavior, mental health, and nutrition and are linked to lower body weight and lost time in school. Often, tooth decay and other dental problems are overlooked.

Children may also experience dental neglect, defined by the American Academy of Pediatric Dentistry (AAPD) as the "willful failure of parent or guardian to seek and follow through with treatment necessary to ensure a level of oral health essential for adequate function and freedom from pain and infection."

Promoting children's oral health from birth can prevent the onset and delay the progression of dental caries. Doing this takes ensuring children have the proper exposure to fluoride, adequate nutrition and limited exposure to sugar, and regular access to oral health professionals. Proper dental care helps children gain nutrition from their food, develop language skills, and improve their overall health. To ensure the healthy development of infants and young children, access to routine dental services should be included in an overall health plan for every child in care.

Ask about children's brushing and flossing habits. Children should brush three times a day and floss at least once, especially at the end of the day. They should be using nonfluoride toothpaste until the child can spit toothpaste out, since swallowing large doses of fluoride can be unhealthy. Ask if children age six months or older have been seen by a dentist and are having regular visits. The AAPD recommends that a primary care physician or health provider refer a child to a dental home as early as six months and by no later than 12 months of age.[40] A referral should also be provided as soon as the baby's first tooth erupts. Ask the agency to report on the initial visit and any recommended follow-up care, as routine follow-up decreases the risk of preventable dental disease. When physical or sexual abuse involving the mouth or dental neglect is suspected, ask whether the child was referred to an appropriate specialist.

The National Council of Juvenile and Family Court Judges encourages judges to ask specific dental health questions during hearings and to coordinate agency efforts to ensure each child's access to a dental home.[41] Relevant questions include:

- Does the child have a dental home and/or access to preventive and treatment services?
- Has the child had a dental exam? When?
- What dental health needs does the child have?
- How are the child's dental health needs being met?
- How often does the child brush? Floss?
- How does the child receive fluoride?
- When is the child's next dental exam scheduled?[42]
- Has the child received sealants?

In addition to health benefits, early preventive care is a sound financial investment. Low-income children who receive their first dental visit by age one are not only less likely to have subsequent restorative or emergency room visits, but their average dental costs are almost 40% lower over a five-year period than those for children who receive their first preventive visit after age one.[43] Communities that fluoridate their water save $38 in dental treatment costs for every $1 spent and giving children sealants reduces treatment costs by preventing cavities.[44] Children who lack periodic preventive dental care are more likely to wait until symptoms (i.e., toothache) become so severe that a visit to the emergency room is warranted. Managing symptoms in an emergency room costs approximately 10 times more than preventive care in a dental office.[45]

Help each child access a dental home.

A "dental home" refers to the ongoing relationship between a patient and a licensed dentist. All aspects of oral health care are delivered in a comprehensive, coordinated, and family-centered way. Like a medical home, the dental home brings together patients, parents, and dental professionals to deliver continuous,

Low-income Children and Dental Health

Low-income children and children of color are at greater risk for tooth decay and untreated cavities:[1]

▶ Poor children are almost twice as likely to have untreated cavities.

▶ Poor children have more severe tooth decay than higher-income youth.

▶ 54.9% of Mexican-American, 43.3% of Black non-Hispanic, and 37.9% of White non-Hispanic children aged 2-11 had untreated tooth decay in their primary teeth.

Source:
1. Beltrán-Aguilar, Eugenio D. et al. *Surveillance for Dental Caries, Dental Sealants, Tooth Retention, Edentulism, and Enamel Fluorosis—United States, 1988–1994 and 1999–2002, 2005.* Available at www.cdc.gov/MMWR/preview/mmwrhtml/ss5403a1.htm.

cost-effective and high-quality oral care. Tooth decay, cavities, and other oral health issues are easily prevented when routine services are provided by a dental home.

A dental home will:

• provide comprehensive oral health care services, including acute and preventive treatment that follow accepted practices and timelines for pediatric dental health;[46]

• conduct an oral disease risk assessment and provide an individualized program for preventive care;

• offer caregivers guidance about growth or development issues (teething and bite development), behavior modification techniques, dietary counseling, and plans in case of emergency dental trauma;[47]

• provide referrals to adult oral care providers when needed, and to other dental specialists, such as endodontists, oral surgeons, orthodontists, and periodontists, when care cannot be provided directly within the dental home.[48]

A referral to a pediatric dentist or a family dentist is the first step in accessing a dental home. It helps to give families a list of providers who participate in the Medicaid program. In addition, local Head Start programs, dental associations, and Internet resources (such as www.aapd.org) are all useful for locating a dental home.[49] Many communities have low-cost dental clinics for low-income children and families.

Innovative Oral Health Programs

▶ **Prevent Abuse and Neglect through Dental Awareness (PANDA) Program**
This program, which started in Missouri but is now running in most states, trains dentists to identify child maltreatment.

▶ **I Smiles**
www.idph.state.ia.us/hpcdp/oral_health_ismile.asp
This statewide program links children to a dental home and is a good example of a coordinated system of care.

▶ **BEST Oral Health Program**
http://baystatehealth.com
(type "Oral Health" in the search box, then click on "BEST Oral Health")
This Massachusetts program addresses oral health issues among vulnerable infants, toddlers, and preschoolers through Early Care & Education Centers.

▶ **Klamath County (Oregon) Early Childhood Cavity Prevention Program**
www.oregon.gov/DHS/ph/oralhealth/programs/klamath.shtml
This initiative links mothers and children to dental care through referrals to local WIC programs.

▶ **Cincy Smiles**
www.cincysmiles.org/
CincySmiles Foundation runs a well-coordinated mobile dental care program in Cincinnati, Ohio, along with several other school- and community-based programs.

▶ **AAP Oral Health Initiative**
www.aap.org/commpeds/dochs/oralhealth/index.cfm
Prepares pediatricians to provide oral health screenings and referrals for young children.

Remove barriers to dental care.

Oral health awareness

Caregivers often lack awareness of the importance of oral health for young children and may be unaware of the need for early and regular oral health care. The priority of oral health can vary due to social, cultural, and economic factors. Dietary practices specific to certain cultures may promote the onset or development of dental caries, while other factors may discourage some groups from pursuing care. Without proper dental care referrals, caregivers may miss the importance of dental care for offsetting and managing dental caries.

There is often a misconception that primary teeth are unimportant since they

Safety Net Providers of Dental Care

Where can low-income children in your community turn for dental care when few dentists will take Medicaid? Safety net providers and services, such as mobile dental programs, community health centers approved by the state or federal government, or dental schools, may fill this need.

Safety net facilities and programs include:

▸ **State-Recognized Safety Net:** These providers include hospitals, diagnostic and treatment centers, community health centers, school-based health centers, and county health departments approved to operate by the state department of health. They receive public funding for oral health services. Dental schools and dental hygiene training programs may also be state-recognized safety net providers if they have explicit policies regarding care for vulnerable populations.

▸ **Federally Recognized Safety Net:** These facilities have been approved as safety net providers by federal agencies such as the Health Resources and Services Administration or Center for Medicare and Medicaid Service. Each agency sets its own administrative and/or service requirements, and recognition provides access to federal funding.

▸ **Community Hospitals:** Although local hospitals and their emergency departments provide medical treatment regardless of ability to pay, these hospitals rarely have the capacity to address routine dental complaints. Young children who come to the emergency room with severe acute dental pain and infection are usually given antibiotics and pain medications to ease their symptoms but may not receive treatment for the underlying disease. Their parents must then take them to a dentist suggested by the hospital, or locate dental care on their own.

▸ **Community & School-Based Centers:** Facilities supported by public and private funders, including school-based (onsite) or school-linked (offsite) health centers, freestanding voluntary health centers, and city and county health centers.

▸ **Head Start and WIC:** Head Start and Early Head Start are required by federal regulation to give clients oral health education, screening, and referrals for treatment. Head Start and the American Academy of Pediatric Dentistry are also working to establish "dental homes" for all children in Head Start.

WIC nutrition programs also provide counseling on oral health and childhood caries prevention and are often co-located in health centers. Local programs that target young at-risk children with health education and social services may also provide oral health services or education.

▸ **Mobile Dental Programs:** Like school-based health centers, mobile programs bring care to children where they are during the day rather than bringing children to care.

Mobile programs include both self-contained vans, and satellite-site programs that bring mobile dental equipment onsite to gyms, auditoriums, and function rooms. Mobile programs may also be used to screen children and identify those who require additional care in a traditional dental setting.

▶ **Medicaid-Focused Private Practices:** Some private practices focus on children on Medicaid. They are easily accessed by public transportation and schedule flexible appointments that accommodate clients' constraints and adjust for high rates of missed appointments. They may engage in more flexible appointment management (e.g., filling in missed appointments by providing more care for children who are present). These practices may provide comprehensive care or limited services.

▶ **Training Programs:** Dental schools, postdoctoral dental residencies, and dental hygiene programs also support the dental safety net.

Source:
Adapted from Edelstein, B.L. *Maximizing Public Dollars in the Provision of Dental Care in New York State.* The Community Health Foundation of Western and Central New York, January 2009.

will eventually fall out, yet they are essential for: biting and chewing food, assisting in speech development, developing jaw bones and facial muscles, reserving space for permanent teeth, and developing self esteem. Additionally, tooth decay in primary teeth is the most reliable predictor of dental caries in permanent teeth.[50]

Access to dental care

Medicaid covers a quarter of all children in this country, but only one-third of enrolled children see a dentist annually. Children enrolled in Medicaid must receive comprehensive dental coverage under EPSDT. Comprehensive dental care is also provided to low-income children through the state Child Health Insurance Program (CHIP). However, dentists' participation in these programs is limited, and access is severely inadequate in many areas.[51]

Fewer than 5% of all U.S. dentists are pediatric dentistry specialists, dentists uniquely trained to manage the behavioral and treatment complexities of children who experience the most severe dental disease. These specialists are commonly located in suburban areas. While more pediatric dentists participate in Medicaid than general dentists, their suburban location is often a barrier for inner-city and rural children. A national survey suggests that fewer than one-in-five dentists participate in Medicaid and far fewer participate significantly.[52]

Due to these barriers, low-income children may need to access dental care through "safety net"[53] providers and services, such as mobile dental programs, community health centers approved by the state or federal government, or dental schools. (See "Safety Net Providers of Dental Care" box.)

Judges can work on several levels to expand access to dental care for children:

- Order that each child in your courtroom have a dental home.
- Advocate for increased Medicaid reimbursement rates for providers.
- Engage state and local dental associations to develop referral and care programs for children in the child welfare system.
- Strengthen relationships with, and state support for, the various safety net providers.

Barriers to Health Care Access

Find out if the child has health insurance.

Many young children in foster care will not receive the medical, dental, developmental, or mental health services they require because of insufficient health insurance coverage. Most children in care are eligible for Medicaid based on their eligibility for Title IV-E foster care funds. Some states also cover non-Title-IV-E eligible children in foster care as an optional category. Children in foster care who are not eligible for Medicaid may be eligible for coverage under the state Children's Health Insurance Program (CHIP). Ensuring all children in care are covered by health insurance will help to maintain continuous health care.

Ask whether the child has health insurance (e.g., Medicaid, private coverage). If the child is uninsured, ask if she is eligible for any programs (e.g., Children's Health Insurance Program) and require that she be enrolled as appropriate. If the child is insured, ask if the coverage is adequate (e.g., does it cover mental health and dental care in addition to routine pediatric care)? If necessary, ask the agency to look into switching to better health insurance, or paying for medical costs that aren't covered by insurance (e.g., broken or lost glasses which Medicaid won't replace, or a wheelchair or ventilator that could take months to procure through Medicaid). Require a supplemental report be filed with the court discussing eligibility, enrollment, and payment of burdensome medical costs before the next court hearing.

Under Medicaid, children are eligible for EPSDT services, which include recommended assessments, screens, and treatment services. Because only Medicaid requires EPSDT services, children without Medicaid coverage may or may not receive such services.

Guidelines for Health Care for Children in Foster Care

This chapter summarizes research and best practices for meeting the health needs of children in care. Two national publications provide additional guidelines:

▶ **Fostering Health: Health Care for Children in Foster Care**
American Academy of Pediatrics (AAP)
Describes practice guidelines for primary care, developmental and mental health care, management of health care, and approaches to child abuse and neglect.

▶ **Standards for Health Care Services for Children in Out-of-Home Care**
Child Welfare League of America (CWLA)
Provides a comprehensive framework to organize physical, developmental, and mental health services for child welfare organizations.

▶ **Additional resource:**
Ensuring the Healthy Development of Foster Children:
A Guide for Judges, Advocates, and Child Welfare Professionals
New York State Permanent Commission on Justice for Children
Asks questions related to the above standards developed by the AAP and the CWLA and gives recommendations for how to meet them. Available at:
www.courts.state.ny.us/ip/justiceforchildren/PDF/ensuringhealthydevelopment.pdf.

Identify other barriers to the child's access to medical services.

The lack of qualified providers who accept Medicaid, or who have experience and knowledge about the health care needs of children in foster care, and the fact that many jurisdictions do not require comprehensive exams, are additional barriers to health care. The high mobility of children in foster care can cause interruptions in insurance when a child moves out of a plan's coverage area. Agencies must make reasonable efforts to meet children's medical and dental health needs. As a judge overseeing the agency's efforts, you can ensure children receive necessary care by ordering the agency to pay the full cost of a visit to a provider outside the child's health insurance plan if there are no qualified providers, or to insure the child under a different health plan with more providers.

Reduced Medicaid spending also prevents many children from accessing services despite insurance coverage. Many states have shifted from a fee-for-service-based Medicaid reimbursement system to a managed care plan, which raises

Red Flags for Health Concerns

The following health conditions are common in young children in foster care. Be familiar with them to quickly identify when a child requires more attention.

Failure to Thrive/Malnutrition:

Failure to thrive (FTT), or growth failure, occurs when a child does not receive sufficient nutrition for proper physical growth and development. FTT is often associated with poverty and may have multiple causes, such as difficulty feeding or underlying medical conditions, including three of the health problems described below (Fetal Alcohol Spectrum Disorders, vertically transmitted infections, and lead poisoning). FTT can also result when a caregiver does not have the means to provide adequate nourishment or does not use available resources. Sometimes, maternal or paternal neglect of a child's nutritional needs stems from mental health and cognitive issues that result in a failure to supply adequate nutrients (nonorganic FTT). Malnutrition in children with FTT not only results in poor growth, but also in long-term deficits in intellectual, social, and psychological functioning. Although not directly linked to FTT, attachment disturbances often accompany the condition, especially nonorganic FTT. Therefore, infants with FTT should be referred for an early childhood developmental and mental health evaluation. Their parents should also be referred for mental health evaluation.

Practice Tips:

▶ Ensure caregivers meet medical recommendations and adhere to treatment plans for children with FTT.

▶ Mandate education for birth and foster parents on the importance of feeding and close social interaction to promote healthy growth and strong attachments.[1]

▶ Mandate a mental health evaluation for the birth parents.

Fetal Alcohol Spectrum Disorders (FASD):

FASD is an umbrella term for three outcomes that can result from a mother drinking during pregnancy (fetal alcohol syndrome, fetal alcohol effects, and alcohol-related neurological disorder).[2] Fetal alcohol syndrome is most known and may be characterized by specific facial features. The other symptoms are common in all the disorders in the FASD spectrum: growth deficits, mental retardation, heart, lung, and kidney problems, chronic ear infections, hyperactivity and behavior problems, attention and memory problems, poor coordination or motor skills delay, difficulty with judgment and reasoning, and learning difficulties.

Practice Tips:

▶ Screen for FASD in all children in foster care.

▶ Require birth parents and foster caregivers to be trained to recognize signs of these disorders.

▶ Ensure an assessment is completed in suspected cases, preferably one conducted by a developmental or behavioral pediatrician or a geneticist. If the assessment reveals a problem, ensure the child's caregiver has the knowledge and support to meet his needs, and the child is receiving early intervention services.

▶ Visit the federal FASD Center for Excellence Web site to learn more about FASD: www.fascenter.samhsa.gov/index.cfm

Because FASD affects learning, especially for young children, assessment is critical to identify services to help a child get ready for school. Obtaining information about a mother's drinking history while pregnant is also vital, since an accurate history of maternal alcohol use is the key to the most conclusive FASD diagnosis.[3]

Vertically Transmitted Infections:

Vertically transmitted infections are infections that a mother passes to her baby, either through the placenta or when the baby passes through the birth canal. Infants can contract viruses, including HIV, hepatitis B, hepatitis C, herpes, HPV (genital warts) and syphilis, among others. A mother may not experience symptoms related to the infection and may unknowingly pass the infection to her child during pregnancy or child birth.

Vertically transmitted infections can be difficult to diagnose because the effects of the infection may not be seen at birth. Complications associated with these infections include damage to the developing brain and other body systems.

▶ Hearing loss may be associated with vertically transmitted infections and may be present at birth or progressively develop and present later in childhood.

▶ Visual problems are also common.

▶ Brain damage can be mild or severe and may cause mental retardation, learning and behavioral disorders, and autism. Special education is frequently required, and early intervention services should also be accessed.

Practice Tip:

▶ Because of the varied effects of vertically transmitted infections, early and periodic hearing, vision, and developmental screens are essential. Make sure screens occur and are repeated at recommended intervals. If necessary, ensure special education or other services are in place.[4] Poor growth is also an early sign of vertically transmitted infections, and calls for screening.

Shaken Baby Syndrome (SBS):

SBS, also called shaken impact syndrome, describes the effects of violently shaking an infant or young child. Children, especially infants, have weak neck muscles, which cannot fully support their heads. When a baby is shaken his brain moves back and forth inside his skull. This movement can cause severe injuries including blindness or eye damage,

Red Flags for Health Concerns (continued)

developmental delay, seizures, paralysis, brain damage, and sometimes death. SBS often occurs in children under two years old, but has been reported in children up to age five.

Although severe cases of SBS may present with signs of head injury, less serious cases may result in symptoms mimicking colic or a viral infection—poor feeding, vomiting, lethargy and irritability—and may delay early attention. Outcomes for children who do not receive medical attention are unknown but they may have learning, motor, or behavior problems later in life with no known cause. When severely injured children survive, they may experience blindness, seizure disorders, severe cognitive impairments, and other serious brain defects.[5]

Practice Tips:

▶ If SBS is suspected, ask if a head injury evaluation has been performed. If not, order one. An adequate assessment of a child with a suspected shaking injury includes a head MRI or CT, an ophthalmology examination to look for retinal hemorrhages, and a skeletal survey to look for subtle fractures of the ribs and long bones that occur with shaking and chest compression. A "babygram" (which gives a single image of the entire infant) is not sufficient; ordering a full range of tests helps establish whether or not the child was the victim of abuse and confirm a diagnosis of SBS.

▶ At the initial hearing, order a thorough investigation of who cared for the child during the seven days before the onset of symptoms.

Lead Poisoning:

Usually caused by environmental lead exposure, lead poisoning can have many long-term effects including decreased intelligence, impaired behavioral development, short stature, hearing problems, and learning difficulties. Children living in poverty, and those in foster care, are at risk for elevated lead levels. Blood screening for elevated lead is the most common way to detect lead poisoning.

Practice Tips:

▶ Ask about lead screening results for all children under age six years or a developmentally delayed child of any age who has a history of pica. Require a lead evaluation if these results are not available.[6]

▶ If the home the child currently lives in (or will live in if case plan goals are met) contains lead-based paint hazards, order lead remediation services.

Respiratory Illness:

Respiratory illnesses are the most common medical problem among children in care. One study reported 19% of children in care as having a respiratory illness. Ear infections make up a large percentage of these infections and can result in long-term problems in hearing, speech, and language development. Asthma and chronic respiratory diseases, such as cystic fibrosis may be less common, but more dangerous for children in care. Respiratory illnesses can also cause breathing difficulties.

Practice Tip:

▶ Make sure any young child with a respiratory illness is evaluated by a medical provider.[7]

Hearing and Vision Problems:

Hearing impairments can hamper a child's speech and language development, personal-social adjustment, and emotional development. As a result, later learning and academic achievement may be limited. Similarly, vision problems may impair school performance, and can signal more significant disease.

Practice Tips:

▶ Hearing, language, and vision should be periodically evaluated in children in foster care because caregivers may be less likely to report subtle abnormalities in these areas. Ask if such screens have been completed regularly coinciding with well-child care visits.

▶ Ask if there is information about the child's newborn hearing screen.

▶ Ask if there is a family history of hearing impairment and ensure this information is relayed to the child's medical home.

▶ Eye exams occur at each well-child visit beginning at birth, but formal visual acuity screening begins successfully around age four.

Sources:

1. Block, R. and N. Krebs. "Failure to Thrive as a Manifestation of Child Neglect." *Pediatrics* 116(5), November 2005, 1234-1236.

2. Hudson, L., L. Burd and K. Kelly. *Recognizing Fetal Alcohol Spectrum Disorders (FASD) in Maltreated Infants, Toddlers and Parents*. Washington, DC: American Bar Association and Zero to Three, forthcoming.

3. *FASD: What Everyone Should Know*. Washington, DC: National Organization on Fetal Alcohol Syndrome. Available at www.nofas.org/resource/factsheet.aspx.

4. Simon, N.P. *Congenital Infections*, Available at www.pediatrics.emory.edu/divisions/neonatology/dpc/conginf.html.

5. American Academy of Pediatrics, Committee on Child Abuse and Neglect. "Shaken Baby Syndrome: Rotational Cranial Injuries—Technical Report." *Pediatrics* 108(1), July 2001, 206-210.

6. Chung, E. et al. "A Comparison of Elevated Blood Lead Levels Among Children Living in Foster Care, Their Siblings, and the General Population." *Pediatrics* 107(5), May 2001, e81-85.

7. Takayama, J., E. Wolfe and K. Coulter. "Relationship Between Reason for Placement and Medical Findings Among Children in Foster Care." *Pediatrics* 101(2), Feb. 1998, 201-207.

concerns about access to comprehensive services, especially mental health services.[54] Many communities lack enough providers who accept Medicaid, and these shortages will worsen as Medicaid cutbacks deepen. Furthermore, continuity of care, which is important for ensuring the healthy development of young children in foster care, may not happen in a managed care system[55] (unless a case manager is assigned).

Closely watching the needs of this population and whether necessary medical care is provided can help counter difficulties that funding restrictions create for public health programs that serve children.

Conclusion

Infants and toddlers in foster care are more likely to have physical health problems than other children. Identifying these problems and intervening early to treat and prevent them is key. Ensuring access to high-quality, consistent health care promotes their optimal physical health and development. You can help ensure that each child in your courtroom achieves optimal physical health by following the guidelines set out in this chapter including each child having a medical and dental home that has all of her relevant medical history and records and provides assessments, indicated follow-up, and preventative and routine care on the schedules advised by the AAP or AAPD. You can also help reduce barriers to good health by ensuring that all children in your courtroom are enrolled in Medicaid or another health insurance program. With effective oversight, court-involved infants and toddlers can grow into healthy children, adolescents, and adults.

Endnotes

1. American Academy of Pediatrics, Task Force on Health Care for Children in Foster Care. *Fostering Health: Health Care for Children and Adolescents in Foster Care*, 2nd ed. Elk Grove Village, IL: American Academy of Pediatrics, 2005.

2. Dicker, S. and E. Gordon. *Ensuring the Healthy Development of Infants in Foster Care: A Guide for Judges, Advocates and Child Welfare Professionals*. Washington, DC: Zero to Three Policy Center, 2004.

3. Ibid.

4. American Academy of Pediatrics, Task Force on Health Care for Children in Foster Care, 2005.

5. Ibid.

6. Ibid.

7. Dicker and Gordon, 2004.

8. Cunningham, M. and E. Cox. "Hearing Assessment in Infants and Children: Recommendations Beyond Neonatal Screening." *Pediatrics* 11(2), February 2003, 436-440.

9. Ibid.

10. Kaye, C. and American Academy of Pediatrics, Committee on Genetics. "Introduction to the Newborn Screening Fact Sheets." *Pediatrics* 118(3), September 2006, 1304-1312. In most states, hearing screens for newborns are required by law or rule; in all but one of the remaining states, the newborn hearing screen is universally offered, but not required. The remaining state offers the test to a select population or upon request.

11. National Institute on Deafness and Other Communication Disorders. "How Medical and Other Health Professionals Can Help Increase the Number of Infants Who Return for a Follow-Up Evaluation." *NIH Pub. No. 98-4291*, August 2003.

12. American Academy of Pediatrics Committee on Practice and Ambulatory Medicine and Bright Futures Steering Committee. "Recommendations for Preventive Pediatric Health Care." *Pediatrics* 120(6), December 2007, 1376.

13. American Speech-Language-Hearing Association. *Speech Sound Disorders: Articulation and Phonological Processes*. Available at www.asha.org/public/speech/disorders/SpeechSound Disorders.htm; American Speech-Language-Hearing Association. *Childhood Apraxia of Speech*. Available at www.asha.org/public/speech/disorders/ChildhoodApraxia.htm; American Speech-Language-Hearing Association. *Stuttering*. Available at www.asha.org/public/speech/disorders/ stuttering.htm; American Speech-Language-Hearing Association. *Vocal Fold Nodules and Polyps*. Available at www.asha.org/public/speech/disorders/NodulesPolyps.htm.

14. American Speech-Language-Hearing Association. *Language-Based Learning Disabilities*. Available at www.asha.org/public/speech/disorders/LBLD.htm.

15. Hagan J.F., J.S. Shaw and P.M. Duncan, eds. *Bright Futures: Guidelines for Health Supervision of Infants, Children, and Adolescents*, 3d ed. Elk Grove Village, IL: American Academy of Pediatrics, 2008.

16. Ibid.

17. Ibid.

18. Ibid.

19. Ibid.

20. American Academy of Pediatrics, Task Force on Newborn and Infant Screening. "Newborn and Infant Hearing Loss: Detection and Intervention." *Pediatrics* 103(2), February 1999, 527-530.

21. American Academy of Pediatrics. "Children's Health Topics: Vision and Hearing." Available at www.aap.org/healthtopics/visionhearing.cfm (last accessed January 30, 2009).

22. American Academy of Pediatrics, Committee on Practice and Ambulatory Medicine and Section on Ophthalmology. "Eye Examination in Infants, Children, and Young Adults by Pediatricians." *Pediatrics* 111(4), April 2003, 902-907.

23. American Academy of Pediatrics Committee on Practice and Ambulatory Medicine and Bright Futures Steering Committee, 2007.

24. American Academy of Pediatrics, Committee on Practice and Ambulatory Medicine and Section on Ophthalmology, 2003.

25. Chung, E. et al. "A Comparison of Elevated Blood Lead Levels Among Children Living in Foster Care, Their Siblings, and the General Population." *Pediatrics* 107(5), May 2001, e81-85.

26. American Academy of Pediatrics Task Force on Health Care for Children in Foster Care, 2005.

27. Ibid.

28. American Academy of Pediatrics, Committee on Early Childhood, Adoption and Dependent Care. "Health Care of Young Children in Foster Care." *Pediatrics* 109(3), March 2002, 536-541.

29. American Academy of Pediatrics Task Force on Health Care for Children in Foster Care, 2005.

30. Osofsky, J.D. et al. "Questions Every Judge and Lawyer Should Ask About Infants and Toddlers in the Child Welfare System." *Technical Assistance Brief*. Reno, NV: National Council of Juvenile and Family Court Judges, 2002.

31. Story, M., K. Holt and D. Sofka, eds. *Bright Futures in Practice: Nutrition*, 2d ed. Arlington, VA: National Center for Education in Maternal and Child Health, 2002.

32. United States Department of Agriculture, Food & Nutrition Services. *WIC at a Glance*, 2005. Available at www.fns.usda.gov/wic/aboutwic/wicataglance.htm.

33. U.S. Department of Health and Human Services, Administration for Children and Families, Administration on Children, Youth and Families, Children's Bureau. *The AFCARS Report: Preliminary FY 2006 Estimates as of January 2008 (14)*. Available at www.acf.hhs.gov/ programs/cb/stats_research/afcars/tar/report14.htm.

34. U.S. Department of Health and Human Services. *Child Welfare Outcomes 2002–2005: Report to Congress*. Available at www.acf.hhs.gov/programs/cb/pubs/cwo05/cwo05.pdf.

35. American Academy of Pediatrics, Committee on Early Childhood, Adoption and Dependent Care, 2002.

36. Ibid.

37. American Academy of Pediatrics, Medical Home Initiatives for Children With Special Needs Project Advisory Committee. "Policy Statement: The Medical Home." *Pediatrics* 110(1), July 2002, 184-186.

38. Edelstein, B.L. "Dental Care Considerations for Young Children." *Special Care Dentist* 22(3), May/June 2002. 11S-25S.

39. American Academy of Pediatrics, Section on Pediatric Dentistry. "Oral Health Risk Assessment Timing and Establishment of the Dental Home." *Pediatrics* 111(5), May 2003, 1113-1116.

40. American Academy of Pediatric Dentistry. *Policy on the Dental Home*. Available at www.aapd.org/media/Policies_Guidelines/P_DentalHome.pdf.

41. Largent, B., C. Lederman and E. Whitney Barnes. "Children's Dental Health: The Next Frontier in Well-Being." *Technical Assistance Brief*. Reno, NV: National Council of Juvenile and Family Court Judges. 2008.

42. Ibid.

43. Savage, M.F. et al. "Early Preventive Dental Visits: Effects on Subsequent Utilization and Costs." *Pediatrics* 114(4), October 2004, e418-23.

44. Sinclair, S.A. and B.L. Edelstein. *Policy Brief: Cost Effectiveness of Preventative Dental Services*. Washington, DC: Children's Dental Health Project, 2005. Available at http://cdhp.org/ downloads/CostEffect.pdf.

45. Pettinato, E., M. Webb and N. Seale. "A Comparison of Medicaid Reimbursement for Non-Definitive Pediatric Dental Treatment in the Emergency Room Versus Periodic Preventive Care." *Pediatric Dentistry* 22(6), November/December 2000, 463-468.

46. American Academy of Pediatric Dentistry. *Policy on the Dental Home*. Available at www.aapd.org/media/Policies_Guidelines/P_DentalHome.pdf.

47. Ibid.

48. Ibid.

49. Largent, et al., 2008.

50. An eight-year study of children ages three-to-five found that children with tooth decay in their primary teeth were three times more likely to develop decay in their permanent teeth. Lil., Y. and W. Wang. "Predicting Caries in Permanent Teeth from Caries in Primary Teeth: An Eight-year Cohort Study." *Journal of Dental Research* 81(8), August 2002, 561-566.

51. Edelstein, 2002.

52. Only a fraction of the dentists surveyed provided more than $10,000 in Medicaid billings per year. Children's Dental Health Project. *Survey of State Medicaid Oral Health Departments on Payment Rates to Dentists, Dentist Participation Levels, Dental Program Administrative*

Issues and Contracting Issues. Washington, DC: Children's Dental Health Project, 1998 (Produced with the National Conference of State Legislatures Forum for State Health Policy Leadership).

53. The Institute of Medicine defines the health care safety net as "Those providers that organize and deliver a significant level of health care and other health-related services to uninsured, Medicaid, and other vulnerable patients" (Institute of Medicine, 2000). Weinick, R.M. and J. Billings. *Introduction: Tools for Monitoring the Health Care Safety Net*. Rockville, MD: Agency for Healthcare Research and Quality, November 2003. Available at www.ahrq.gov/data/safetynet/intro.htm.

54. 42 U.S.C. §1396(a)(10) and (43)(2000); 42 U.S.C. §1396(d)(a)(4)(B) (2000); 42 U.S.C. §1396(r).

55. DiGiuseppe, D. and D. Christakis. "Continuity of Care for Children in Foster Care." *Pediatrics* 11(3), March 2003, e208-e213.

Addressing Early Mental Health and Devlopmental Needs

Addressing Early Mental Health and Developmental Needs

Factors that Influence Social-Emotional Development of Young Children

▶ Understand how child maltreatment affects children's development.

▶ Ensure placements for very young children provide long-term stability and promote healthy attachments.

Mental Health Assessment and Services

▶ Order an immediate screening of the child's mental health issues.

▶ Require a screening to identify developmental delays and disorders.

▶ Ensure the comprehensive mental health assessment is initiated within 30-60 days of placement.

▶ Order a reassessment of the child's mental health status during placement.

▶ Ensure a continuum of services is offered to each child.

▶ Ensure frequent parent-child contact.

▶ Ensure frequent sibling contact.

▶ Ensure the mental health and emotional needs of the parent(s) are assessed and appropriate services are provided.

▶ Order a determination of the intensity and type of services required to meet the family's needs.

▶ Order an assessment to determine whether the child and parent would benefit from Child-Parent Psychotherapy.

chapter 3

▶ Order an assessment of whether the child and parent would benefit from Parent-Child Interaction Therapy (PCIT).

▶ Ensure services respond to the needs of different ethnic and cultural groups.

Early Care and Education

▶ Ensure children participate in positive early childhood learning experiences.

▶ Carefully consider the availability and quality of early care and education settings.

From birth, babies look to trusted adults to meet their needs. When their needs are met, babies thrive. When their needs are not met, their social-emotional development (mental health) is compromised. In either case, babies' brains are learning what to expect from the world, and whatever happens during the first three years becomes part of the brain's hard wiring. The zero-to-three age range is the time when the greatest amount of development occurs in the brain.

Even though the brain is constantly growing, changing, and forming new connections during early childhood, recovering lost connections becomes much harder with age. Babies are born with just a portion of the connections they will later develop. Through their relationships with caregivers and trusted adults who talk to, play with, and comfort them, the brain will build many connections. In fact, a newborn's brain produces many more connections than will be needed during childhood. The connections that are not used or needed become weaker and are eventually tossed away, or pruned from the brain.

Research shows that removing a child from a neglectful home after age four offers little opportunity to recover the initial attachment.[1] That is why early maltreatment is potentially so damaging. The sooner a child is able to develop a consistent, positive attachment with a primary caregiver, the more likely he will develop the confidence and intellectual curiosity to succeed throughout childhood and as an adult. The key to healthy social and emotional development is positive and consistent early experiences with loving caregivers. Supportive interventions for children and their parents and quality early child care and educational experiences are also important to promoting children's positive mental health.

As a judge, you can guard the mental health of very young children by making sure that:

- placement decisions are made wisely at the outset that promote long-term stability and healthy child-caregiver attachments,
- ties are maintained with birth parents and siblings through frequent quality visits, and
- permanency decisions respect the bonds children have forged in out-of-home care.

Factors that Influence Social-Emotional Development of Young Children

Understand how child maltreatment affects children's development.

In very young children, the terms *social-emotional development* and *infant mental health* are used interchangeably. Social-emotional development describes "the

Common Mental Health and Developmental Disorders of Infancy and Early Childhood

The Diagnostic Classification of Mental Health and Developmental Disorders of Infancy and Early Childhood (DC:0-3) was first published in 1994 by Zero To Three to address the need for a systematic, developmentally based approach to the classification of mental health and developmental disorders in the first four years of life. The DC:0-3R was published in 2005 and builds on the tradition of the first version. DC:0-3R uses a multiaxial system with five major classifications of disorders and they are:

▶ **Axis I:** The infant's primary diagnosis. Examples are posttraumatic stress disorder, affective disorders and eating behavior disorders.

▶ **Axis II:** Disorders related to the caregiver-child relationship. Examples of categories include angry/hostile, over-/underinvolved, verbally, physically, or sexually abusive relationship disorders.

▶ **Axis III:** Medical and/or developmental conditions including developmental language disorder, failure to thrive, and cerebral palsy.

▶ **Axis IV:** Acute and chronic stressors in the child's environment. Examples are parental psychopathology and parental conflict.

▶ **Axis V:** The young child's current functional and emotional level of adaptation.

Source:
Diagnostic Classification of Mental Health and Developmental Disorders of Infancy and Early Childhood (DC: 0-3). Washington, DC: Zero to Three Press, 1994; *Diagnostic Classification of Mental Health and Developmental Disorders of Infancy and Early Childhood: Revised Edition (DC: 0-3R).* Washington, DC: Zero to Three Press, 2005.

developing capacity of the child from birth through five years of age to form close and secure adult and peer relationships; experience, regulate, and express emotions in socially and culturally appropriate ways; and explore the environment and learn—all in the context of family, community, and culture."[2]

Healthy emotional and psychological development of infants and young children requires that the child have a relationship with a nurturing, protective adult who fosters trust and security. This is an **attachment relationship**. A young child forms attachments during the period of early brain development, which sets the framework for emotional development. The professional literature[3] identifies four types of attachment relationships:[4]

• **Secure attachment:** The child trusts that her parents are consistently available. When the child is frightened or unsure about something, she

Autism Spectrum Disorders

What are Autism Spectrum Disorders?

Autism Spectrum Disorders (ASD), most commonly diagnosed in young children, fall in the category of difficulty in relating and communicating.[1] An estimated 1 in 150 children are on the autism spectrum, which has prompted researchers to describe the disorder as "an urgent public health issue."[2] Typically diagnosed by three years of age, ASD can be recognized in children as young as two years. Although symptoms present differently in individual children, many will manifest problems in social interaction, verbal and nonverbal communication, and repetitive behaviors or interests.[3]

General Indicators of ASD

▶ **Social Indicators:** Typically, developing infants are born ready to be in relationships with adults and primary caregivers. The parent-infant relationship helps form the foundation for healthy infant and toddler social-emotional development. Some very young children with ASD have difficulty interacting and sustaining eye contact with parents and caregivers. As these young children grow and develop, their passiveness, self-isolation, and resistance to human affection often becomes more pronounced. They may also become attached to a particular toy or object to the point that if the toy or object is moved or lost the child will become very upset, lose control, and have difficulty calming down. These children may:

- ▶ not smile very often,
- ▶ seem hearing impaired,
- ▶ lose social skills apparent earlier in development, and
- ▶ crave rituals and/or order to their activities.

▶ **Communication Problems:** One of the first sounds very young infants make is babbling. By the first year babbling typically develops into words. Some children diagnosed with ASD never speak, others babble for the first few months and then stop. Still others are delayed in developing language. Some children develop echolalia, a language disorder in which the young child parrots everything he/she hears. Although many children repeat everything they hear, this phase usually ends around three years of age. Many ASD children:

- ▶ do not respond to their names, and
- ▶ lose language skills apparent earlier in development.

Any parent or foster caregiver who suspects a problem with a young child should seek Early Intervention screening and a diagnosis as soon as possible. The American Academy of Pediatrics recommends autism-specific screenings at 18 months with a follow-up at 24 months, and whenever a concern is raised (in addition to general developmental screenings at 9, 18, and 30 months).[4] Judges should ask whether such screening has occurred. Early screening and diagnosis is important for ASD children because the sooner a child is diagnosed, the sooner services can begin to support them.

Sources:

1. *Diagnostic Classification of Mental Health and Developmental Disorders of Infancy and Early Childhood: Revised Edition (DC:0-3R).* Washington, DC: Zero to Three Press, 2005.

2. Johns Hopkins Bloomberg School of Public Health. "CDC Releases New Data on the Prevalence of Autism Spectrum Disorders: First and Largest Multi-site Study Provides Baseline for Future Comparisons." *Public Health News Center,* 2007. Available at www.jhsph.edu/publichealthnews/articles/2007/lee_autism.html.

3. U.S. Department of Health and Human Services. *Autism Spectrum Disorders: Pervasive Developmental Disorders.* National Institutes of Health, National Institute of Mental Health, NIH Publication No. 08-5511, 2004. Available at www.nimh.nih.gov/health/publications/autism/complete-publication.shtml.

4. Hagan J.F., J.S. Shaw and P.M. Duncan, eds. *Bright Futures: Guidelines for Health Supervision of Infants, Children, and Adolescents,* 3d ed. Elk Grove Village, IL: American Academy of Pediatrics, 2008, 226.

looks to her parents for reassurance. If the parent is calm, the child is no longer frightened. She may move closer to the parent to touch base but then will return to whatever activity she was engaged in before the threat.

- **Anxious-ambivalent attachment:** The child cannot count on his parents to respond consistently. Sometimes the parent is nurturing and sometimes she is not. The child uses two coping strategies interchangeably—clinginess and feigned independence—to demonstrate his insecurity.

- **Anxious-avoidant insecure attachment:** The child has learned that the parent is not there for her. She behaves as though she has no need for the parent's attention.

- **Disorganized attachment:** This form of attachment is associated with children who have been physically abused and is the most difficult to treat. Such a child has no strategy for dealing with his parents' failure to protect and nurture him. He attempts proximity with his parent in odd ways such as approaching her backwards or simply falling in a heap near her.

Insecure attachment underlies later mental health problems, substance addiction, homelessness, and criminal activity.[5] Especially for children in foster care, who often have unstable relationships with adults, understanding and promoting attachment is critical to ensuring healthy emotional and mental development.

Infants and toddlers living with families dealing with substance use disorders are also at risk for developing mental health disorders.[6] For example, they may cry for long periods, seem unable to soothe themselves or be soothed, have trouble sleeping and eating, and withdraw from adults and peers. These children find

Biological Factors Affecting Social-Emotional Development

▶ **Premature Birth:** Any birth that occurs before the 37th week of pregnancy is considered preterm. The more prematurely a baby is born the greater the health risks. Babies born very prematurely often have breathing, digestive, and brain problems and are at high risk for death in the first few days of life. Premature babies may continue to have developmental delays and learning problems that will affect them throughout their lives.

▶ **Low Birth Weight and Small for Gestational Age:** Infants weighing under 5½ pounds at birth are *low birth weight* and are at increased risk for other health problems and developmental delays.[1] *Small for gestational age* infants have birth weights below the third percentile for gestational age. Very small infants have great difficulty regulating their behavior in response to changes in emotional stimulation. A fussy baby is normally soothed when a parent gently holds him and rocks, or talks softly to her and gently rubs her back, but very small infants are not able to benefit from these soothing techniques and their emotional distress continues unabated. This early regulatory difficulty may be linked to the later diagnosis of attention deficit hyperactivity disorder.[2]

▶ **Neurobehavioral Problems:** During the first few days of life, drug-exposed infants experience tremors and irritability.[3] They may also have diarrhea, vomiting, and even seizures. Some newborns are lethargic, and many are easily distracted and overstimulated. Others display poor quality of movement and self-regulation.

Sources:

1. Bada, H. S. et al. "Gestational Cocaine Exposure and Intrauterine Growth: Maternal Lifestyle Study." *Obstetrics & Gynecology* 100, 2002, 916–924.

2. Committee on Integrating the Science of Early Childhood Development, National Research Council and Institute of Medicine. *From Neurons to Neighborhoods: The Science of Early Childhood Development*. Edited by Shonkoff, J.P and D.A. Philllips. Board on Children, Youth, and Families, Commission on Behavioral and Social Sciences and Education. Washington, DC: National Academy Press, 2000, 349.

3. Lester, B. M. et al. "Methamphetamine Exposure: A Rural Early Intervention Challenge." *Zero To Three* 26(4), 2006, 30–36.

it difficult to develop and sustain strong connections with adults and others, leading to attachment disorders that may affect their ability to form relationships, take risks, explore the world around them, and learn.[7]

Researchers estimate that 30 to 70% of the children witnessing domestic violence also experience child abuse as a result.[8] The impact on young children can be devastating, as many never learn to expect their parents to protect them and ensure their well-being.[9] Because the parents cannot make the child safe, and indeed, contribute to the child's insecurity, the child is caught in a terrible dilemma: try to stay away from parents who might harm him or seek parental comfort and protection when it is unclear whether the parents will provide them. Children exposed to this kind of stress are likely to have a disorganized attachment relationship with their parents.[10] The child's response to this violence can lead to a clinical diagnosis of traumatic stress disorder, which includes these symptoms:

- experiencing the traumatic events over and over through ritualistic play, flashbacks, and nightmares;
- becoming distressed when exposed to anything that reminds the child of the trauma;
- losing previously acquired skills (e.g., a child who had been toilet trained has repeated accidents);
- blunting personality: the child stops expressing emotion, interacting with people, or carrying out normal play activities;
- becoming hypervigilent: the child is easily startled, cannot relax or fall asleep, and wakes up frequently at night;
- displaying behavioral symptoms that appear after the traumatic events (e.g., aggression toward people or animals, separation anxiety, other new fears).

We would like to believe it is never too late to rehabilitate a child who has suffered harmful early childhood experiences. However, the science of early childhood tells us that the initial attachment is critical to protect against future inadequacies in relationship building and behavioral control. When children experience long periods without forming this initial attachment, or repeatedly begin and end relationships, they become less and less likely to achieve it.

Ensure placements for very young children provide long-term stability and promote healthy attachments.

Stable placements with loving adults and predictable nurturing routines promote healthy attachments for very young children. By the time child protective services (CPS) intervenes, these essentials are likely to be lacking. Helping the child overcome the maltreatment that brought CPS into the picture requires careful planning, and the child needs to be protected from multiple moves between caregivers. To do this, extended family members need to be identified as close to the removal as possible, ideally before the child is removed. Ask caseworkers to describe efforts to identify extended family caregivers in the first week after the case comes to them.

In the event that extended family members are not available or not appropriate as caregivers at the time of removal, a foster-to-adopt home should be selected. Placements should be evaluated to ensure that they support the mental health

Red Flags[1]

Children who are too young to speak communicate in other ways. Even very young infants tell us when they are suffering. In their first year of life, children react to trauma through the disruption of normal biological rhythms and sensorimotor responses outside of what would typically be expected.[2] Mental health problems are often reflected in physiologic responses to stress and a pattern of behavior that includes multiple episodes or symptoms. They should be treated seriously.

An infant under chronic stress may respond with:

▶ apathy—lose interest in the world (caregivers cannot elicit a smile);
▶ poor feeding—refusal to eat or an insatiable appetite (failure to thrive and morbid obesity are possible outcomes);
▶ develop symptoms like vomiting or skin rashes for which there is no detectable diagnosis;
▶ withdrawal.

More acute stress may lead to various responses:

▶ inconsolable crying;
▶ temper tantrums;
▶ aggressive behaviors;
▶ inattention and withdrawal.

A young child's response to stress may include:

▶ excessive day dreaming;
▶ disengagement;
▶ opposition;
▶ defiance.

Repeated experiences can lead to dysregulation of the areas of the brain that control motor activity and anxiety. Children can consequently display:

▶ motor hyperactivity;
▶ out-of-control and accident-prone behavior, or overly cautious movements and activities;
▶ anxiety;
▶ mood swings;
▶ impulsive behavior;
▶ sleep problems;
▶ caring for self, siblings, or parent beyond what is expected for such a young child;
▶ taking responsibility for abusive behavior in play ("If only I hadn't skinned my knee, Daddy wouldn't have hit Mommy."); and

▶ oversexualized behavior (excessive masturbation, inappropriate touching, or body rubbing).

Sources:
1. Adapted from American Academy of Pediatrics, Committee on Early Childhood, 2000.
2. Lieberman, A.F et al. "Violence in Infancy and Early Childhood: Relationship-Based Treatment and Evaluation." *Interventions for Children Exposed to Violence.* Edited by A.F. Lieberman and R. DeMartino. New Brunswick, NJ: Johnson & Johnson Pediatric Institute, 2006, 65-83.

needs of young children. However, foster parents need special training to understand their dual roles as coach to the parents when reunification is the permanency goal, and as adoptive parents if the biological parents are not able to overcome the problems that led them into the child welfare system. Ask about the training provided to the foster parents to prepare them to care for very young children and about supportive services to help the family address the child's emotional needs.

Make sure all parties understand that placement decisions are being closely examined and any changes in placement will be reviewed in court. Also ensure concurrent permanency planning begins on day one to engage both parents and other potential permanency resources in supporting the child's healthy development. Cases should progress without delay when a permanency plan changes.

Effect of Cognitive and Developmental Delays on Young Children's Mental Health

While the effect of insecure attachment on the social-emotional development of very young children is significant, cognitive and developmental delays are other factors that can play a major role. Before children are born, their parents are already influencing their lives. If their mothers drink alcohol, take drugs (either recreational or prescription), smoke cigarettes, fail to eat enough healthy food, are exposed to chronic stress, or are victims of violence or environmental toxins, the children are at an elevated risk for several developmental challenges that affect their social-emotional development. Common biological problems in babies that often lead to developmental delays are premature birth, low birth weight, and neurobehavioral problems. Cognitive problems in toddlers and young children such as autism can lead to difficult or insecure attachments with caregivers and other trusted adults. For parents who have looked forward to nurturing a relationship with their infant or toddler, these signs can be very upsetting and cause parents and very young children much tension and stress. Parents who expected to bond with an infant or toddler who appears nonresponsive may feel deeply disappointed and at a loss as to how to respond.

Mental Health Assessment and Services

Order an immediate screening of the child's mental health issues.

The initial mental health screening should occur within 24 hours of removal. The primary purpose is to identify and provide services for any emergency mental health needs. Any biological factors affecting very young children's mental health should be evaluated during the initial mental health assessment and follow-up screenings. Young children who are removed from their caregivers may require an immediate intervention to address acute separation issues. Early efforts to prevent, identify, and support mental health issues are crucial for young children entering foster care. Whenever removal occurs, responding to the child's needs first requires a comprehensive evaluation of their social-emotional health and development. Quality assessments are key to uncovering early signs of emotional and mental distress so that services can begin to address them. Treatment and interventions should be trauma-informed and evidence-based.

The American Academy of Child and Adolescent Psychiatry (AACAP) and the Child Welfare League of America (CWLA) recommend an immediate mental health screening followed by a comprehensive mental health evaluation for all children who are removed from their primary caregivers due to suspected abuse, neglect, or caregiver impairment.[11] A qualified mental health professional, such as a psychiatric nurse practitioner, who uses recognized clinical tools and has training and experience with very young children should conduct the evaluation.

Require a screening to identify developmental delays and disorders.

The Child Abuse Prevention and Treatment Act of 2003 (CAPTA) requires that children who are the subjects of substantiated child maltreatment complaints receive a screening to identify developmental delays. If the child has developmental delays, she is eligible for a wide range of services authorized by Part C of the Individuals with Disabilities Education Act (IDEA) (see Part C box). Part C screening provides a thorough picture of a child's developmental status. Evaluating the child's social-emotional health is one important component of that assessment that may be overlooked if the agency responsible for implementation lacks

Part C of the Individuals with Disabilities Education Act[1]

Congress established the Part C program under the IDEA in 1986 to address an "urgent and substantial need." The purpose of Part C is to:

▶ enhance the development of infants and toddlers with disabilities;

▶ reduce education costs by reducing the need for special education through early intervention services;

▶ minimize the likelihood of institutionalization; and

▶ enhance the capacity of families to meet their children's needs.

Amendments to the Child Abuse and Prevention Treatment Act (CAPTA) from 2003 require states to develop procedures to ensure that all children under age three who are involved in a substantiated case of abuse or neglect are referred to Part C services.

The IDEA amendments of 2004 require Part C services for all children who have been maltreated or exposed to prenatal substance and alcohol use or domestic violence. This legislation opened a window of opportunity for getting developmental assessments and treatment for infants and toddlers who have been abused or neglected. However, although Part C is a federal requirement, many local jurisdictions are not yet aware of the Part C program in their states.

For eligible children, Part C services include:[2]

▶ family training, counseling, and home visits;

▶ nursing, health, and nutrition services;

▶ service coordination;

▶ medical services for diagnostic or evaluation purposes;

▶ occupational and physical therapy;

▶ psychological and social work services;

▶ vision, orientation and mobility services;

▶ speech-language pathology services;

▶ transportation services; and

▶ age-appropriate special education instruction.

To learn more about Part C of the IDEA, visit:

www.childwelfare.gov/systemwide/service_array/development/childwelfare.cfm

Sources:

1. Hudson, L. et al. *Healing the Youngest Children: Model Court-Community Partnerships*. Washington, DC: American Bar Association Center on Children and the Law & Zero to Three Policy Center, 2007.

2. Santucci, R. et al. *Special Education: Grant Programs Designed to Serve Children Ages 0-5*. Washington, DC: United States General Accounting Office, 2002, 8. Available at www.gao.gov/new.items/d02394.pdf.

expertise in infant mental health. If a thorough Part C assessment is available, a separate mental health assessment may not be necessary.

The American Academy of Pediatrics (AAP) recommends that pediatricians screen all children for developmental disorders at every pediatric visit.[12] When developmental risks are identified, the health care provider should administer a developmental screening tool and determine whether referrals for further evaluation or services are necessary. In addition to routine surveillance, the AAP recommends all children, irrespective of risk for developmental concerns, undergo formal developmental screening at 9, 18, and 30 month visits. Whenever any screening tool identifies potential issues, referrals for further evaluation and services should be made.

Children receiving common early intervention services (e.g., speech, information processing, and other cognitive and motor functions) have a higher risk for behavioral and mental health disorders.[13] When mental health services are provided under Part C, "relationship-based and family-focused intervention strategies [should be used] by early intervention personnel, regardless of professional discipline or the service being provided."[14] Strategies include:

- working with the parent and child together;
- educating parents about things they can expect in their child's behavior;
- building on parents' strengths to enhance their ability to care for their child;
- offering opportunities for the parent and child to interact positively; and
- helping the parent explore their feelings about the child and about being a parent.[15]

Ensure the comprehensive mental health assessment is initiated within 30-60 days of placement.

Typically, when a child is removed from the caregivers and placed in out-of-home care, he is suddenly separated from all things familiar—his home, community, educational setting, caregivers, family, and friends. This experience causes grief that can impair new attachments and the success of the out-of-home placement. Ensuring an early and comprehensive evaluation of a child's mental health needs by a professional familiar with the social and emotional needs of children in care will help address the young child's distress. Ask about the results of the mental health screening that was done before placement. If one has not been completed, order one.

A comprehensive assessment should occur within 30-60 days of placement. The timing of this evaluation should be guided by any mental health needs identified in the initial screening. The initial evaluation and the comprehensive assessment should focus on the potential psychological consequences of removal, with or without the presence of symptoms that support a psychiatric diagnosis.

While the focus of this chapter is mental health, it bears repeating that a full assessment should include a thorough physical exam and developmental evaluation. Delays in cognitive and motor functioning can be clues to previous maltreatment. For example, an infant who cannot track objects with her eyes may have suffered an eye injury.[16]

Learning about infants and toddlers occurs most successfully in conditions that create the least stress for them. Assessments of very young children should occur in familiar settings, whenever possible. The child should never be separated from the primary caregiver (e.g., foster parent, birth parent, kinship care provider) during the evaluation. A thorough assessment should be conducted over two or three sessions to accommodate the child's rapidly changing moods, health, and comfort.

Many instruments and procedures are used to evaluate young children. These instruments are used together to paint a complete picture of the child's mental health. The differing approaches highlight:

- infant development and functioning
- the social-emotional domain
- the child's adaptive skills
- parent-child interaction

Order a reassessment of the child's mental health status during placement.

During placement, the emotional and mental health needs of children in foster care will change, varying with the child's age, developmental stage, and circumstances. For this reason, children's emotional and mental health status should be periodically reassessed during placement. For children with particular mental health needs, reassessment should occur at appropriate intervals. An assessment occurring very soon after placement may portray the child as having very different behaviors than one conducted after the child has had time to adapt to the changed situation.

Consistent surveillance is required to detect developmental delays early. Health providers who know about the developmental needs of children play a key role in identifying potential problems for maltreated children. Young children who have been maltreated should receive a full mental health evaluation no later than one month after entering care[17] and every six months thereafter. These assessments should address the effects of maltreatment and the quality of the child's placement experience. The evaluators should be looking at how the child

Commonly Used Developmental Screening Tools

Developmental Screening Tools Using Information from Parents

▶ **Ages & Stages Questionnaires (ASQ) Second Edition**
The ASQ uses drawings and simple directions to help parents elicit and indicate children's language, personal-social, motor, and cognition skills. The ASQ is tied to well-child visits. A newly developed Ages and Stages Questionnaire: Social Emotional (ASQ:SE) helps screen for emotional and behavioral problems in children 6–60 months of age.

▶ **Parents' Evaluation of Developmental Status (PEDS)**
PEDS is a 10-question screening and surveillance tool designed to detect and address a wide range of developmental issues including behavioral and mental health problems. Parents can complete it in just a few minutes, and it promotes parent-provider collaboration and family-centered practice. PEDS identifies when to refer, screen further or refer for additional screening, or monitor development, behavior, and academic progress. Research shows use of PEDS improves positive parenting practices and satisfaction with services.

▶ **PEDS: Developmental Milestones (PEDS:DM)**
PEDS:DM uses six-to-eight items per well-visit that address different developmental domains: fine motor, gross motor, expressive language, receptive language, self-help, social-emotional, and for older children reading and math. The PEDS:DM can be used with or without PEDS but in combination better helps meet the AAP's 2006 policy statement on early detection.

▶ **Infant-Toddler Checklist for Language and Communication**
Parents complete 24 multiple-choice questions that focus on social aspects of their child's language development. Scores are produced for the child's social, speech, and symbolic communication skills. It does not screen for motor milestones.

Developmental Screens Requiring Direct Elicitation of Children's Skills

▶ **Bayley Infant Neurodevelopmental Screener (BINS)**
The BINS assesses neurological processes (reflexes and tone); neurodevelopmental skills (movement and symmetry); and developmental accomplishments (imitation, and language).

▶ **Brigance Screens-II**
Separate forms each cover a 12-month age range to screen speech-language, motor, readiness, and general knowledge skills, and for the youngest age group,

social-emotional skills. All screens use direct elicitation and observation except the Infant and Toddler Screen, which can be administered by parent report. This screen is widely used in educational settings.

▶ **Battelle Developmental Inventory Screening Test (BDIST)**
BDIST uses a combination of direct assessment, observation, and parental interview to screen receptive and expressive language, fine and gross motor, adaptive, personal-social, and cognitive/academic skills.

Behavioral/Emotional/Mental Health Screening Tools

▶ **Eyberg Child Behavior Inventory (ECBI)/Sutter Eyberg Student Behavior Inventory Revised (SESBI-R)**
The ECBI consists of 36 short statements of common acting-out behaviors. Parents rate each item for frequency of occurrence (referred to as intensity) on a one–to-seven scale and then indicate whether the behavior is a problem for them. A single score is produced to suggest the presence of disruptive, externalizing behavior problems (e.g., disorders of attention, conduct, oppositional-defiance). The SESBI-R works in a similar way but uses teachers as the informant.

▶ **Pediatric Symptom Checklist (PSC)**
The PSC consists of 35 short statements of externalizing (conduct, attention, etc.) and internalizing (depression, anxiety, adjustment, etc.) problem behaviors.

Sources:
Smith, P.K. "Chapter 3: Early Intervention Using Standardized Developmental Screening Tools." *Enhancing Child Development Services in Medicaid Managed Care; A Best Clinical and Administrative Practices Toolkit for Medicaid.* Hamilton, NJ: Center for Health Care Strategies, Inc., 2005. Available at www.chcs.org/usr_doc/Toolkit.pdf;
Frances P. Glascoe, MD. "Commonly Used Screening Tools." *Developmental Behavioral Pediatrics Online* (AAP). Available at www.dbpeds.org/articles/detail.cfm?textid=539.

expresses emotions, his ability to regulate himself (e.g., Can he calm himself after a disappointment?), his self awareness, and his relationships with the primary caregivers in his life.

Ensure a continuum of services is offered to each child.

Identifying mental health needs is the first step in promoting the emotional and mental health of young children in care. Given their complex prior experiences, and the diversity of placement options, children's needs are best met through a complement of mental health services. Services should permit the child to remain in the least restrictive, but also safe, community-based environment and should encourage *voluntary* family participation at all stages.[18]

All children should receive individualized service planning to address all their needs including their mental health and emotional needs. Plans should include:

- services that focus on the interests, values, and goals of the child and family;
- targeted assessment of the mental health needs of the child and services and supports to help the family support the child;
- a concurrent permanency plan to reduce the need for multiple placement changes by preparing foster parents to serve as adoptive parents if reunification is not possible;
- informal and formal services such as visit coaching or child-parent psychotherapy, and opportunities to participate in community activities (e.g., Early Head Start, faith-based organizations);
- assessments of progress toward identified goals.

Review the child's individualized service plan to ensure it incorporates supports that meet identified needs. Services should continue when a child is reunified with his family or another permanency plan is implemented. If no services have been required while the child is in care, his needs should be reassessed at each hearing and any necessary services should begin at that time.

Ensure frequent parent-child contact.[19]

Professionals working with very young children in foster care often do not understand the extent of the child's distress over being removed from the parent and placed in a strange environment. Remember that very young children grieve the loss of a relationship. Even though the parent has maltreated the child, she or he is the only parent the child has known, and separation evokes strong and painful emotional reactions.[20] The younger the child and the longer the period of uncertainty and separation from the primary caregiver, the greater the risk of harm to the child.[21] Maintaining consistent contact between the child and his or her parents and siblings is critical unless visits would harm the child.[22] In fact, parent-child contact is the number one indicator of reunification.[23] Family contact and interaction is important and the relationship between the foster family and biological family can be crucial.

Because physical proximity with the caregiver is central to the attachment process for infants and toddlers,[24] an infant should ideally spend time with the parent(s) daily, and a toddler should see the parent(s) at least every two to three days.[25] To reduce the trauma of sudden separation, the first parent-child visit should occur as soon as possible and no later than 48 hours after the child is removed from the home.[26]

Visits should promote parent-child attachment and be an opportunity to model good parenting skills. The length and frequency of visits should reflect the child's developmental stages and gradually increase as the parent shows she is able to respond to her child's cues in consistent and nurturing ways, soothe her child, and attend to her child's needs. During the initial phase, limiting visits to one-to-two hours allows the parent to experience small successes without becoming over-whelmed. By the transition phase, as the family approaches reunification, unsu-pervised all-day, overnight, and weekend visits should be completed.[27]

A young child's emotional dysregulation following a visit does not necessarily mean the parent did something harmful during the visit.[28] Visitation can be ex-tremely upsetting for children, and it is important to understand the developmen-tal context of their feelings and behaviors. Very young children cannot understand the separation, and they tend to respond with bewilderment, sadness, and grief. During visits, they may cling or cry, act out, or withdraw from their parent. At the end of a visit, when another separation is imminent, they may become confused, sad, or angry. Following visits, infants and toddlers may show regressive behav-iors, depression, physical symptoms, or behavioral problems. Foster caregivers may need information to help them understand and support young children who are distressed after a visit.

Parents also find visits to be a time of emotional upheaval, particularly during the first phase of placement. Parents often experience pain and sadness resulting from the separation. They may feel shame, guilt, depression, denial that there is a problem, anger, and/or worry about the child. During the first visits, the parent is likely to be awkward, tense, and uncertain. Visit coaches, caseworkers, and fos-ter parents should help the parent process her emotions and help her interact with her child.[29]

Ensure frequent sibling contact.

The Fostering Connections to Success and Increasing Adoptions Act of 2008[30] ad-dresses many issues that promote permanency and affect the health and well-being of very young children in foster care, including placing greater priority on keeping siblings together. While placements that can accommodate a very young child's siblings should be sought, it may be necessary to separate siblings due to the special needs or circumstances of the very young child. When siblings are not placed together, the importance of siblings to the young child should not be min-imized, especially if there is an established bond. Ensure frequent sibling visits and opportunities to maintain the sibling bond, especially for toddlers and preschoolers who may perceive their older siblings as caregivers.

Ensure the mental health and emotional needs of the parent(s) are assessed and appropriate services are provided.

Because children's early social-emotional development depends on their parents' health and well-being,[31] issues that undermine the parents' sense of safety and belonging will harm the young child's mental health. Infants react to trauma as it is manifested through their parents' lack of availability to provide them nurturing care.[32] Promoting a family-centered approach to mental health assessments and services will uncover many family needs that can be addressed early in the child welfare case.

Children thrive to the extent that their parents provide consistent nurturing care. Parents whose lives are consumed by substance abuse, mental illness, domestic violence, a history of childhood trauma, compromised cognitive functioning, or poverty cannot provide the care their very young children need because they are often distracted by their own issues. With proper interventions and support, they can address these problems and work toward resuming care of their children.

Substance Abuse

Parents with addiction problems may be unable to provide consistent emotional and psychological attention to infants and toddlers because they are preoccupied by their chemical addiction. Primary caregivers who are chemically dependent are likely to have experienced maltreatment as children.[33] They are often unable to provide the comfort, security, and consistent care infants and toddlers need to regulate their behaviors and emotions. Parents with addiction issues are also likely to have been exposed to alcohol in utero which brings with it a host of possible disabilities (e.g., fetal alcohol spectrum disorders; neurobehavioral problems). Parents with addiction problems should complete a parenting course focused on these issues.

Mental Illness

Parents with mental illnesses run the gamut. Many are competent and manage their parenting responsibilities appropriately and without help, while others are good parents with some assistance. Some lack sufficient parenting skills and others are abusive, neglectful, or both.[34] Psychopathology among parents of young children is often linked to maltreatment. For new parents, postpartum depression, post traumatic stress disorder, depression, and anxiety can interfere with their ability to care for their newborns. Maternal depression and other psychiatric problems (e.g., hostile personality, explosiveness) are linked to abuse of infants.[35] Research documents high rates of psychopathology among biological parents who maltreat their young children. Children of psychotic parents often experience confusion over reality. If no other caregiver is available, they can get lost in the psychotic world of the one available parent. More recently, high rates of psychiatric illness have been identified among foster and kinship parents.[36]

Infants with chronically depressed mothers will often withdraw from social interactions, jeopardizing their social-emotional development. As they get older, these children are likely to lack self control, behave aggressively towards other children, and experience school difficulties that can lead to grade retention and dropping out of school.[37]

If services to the parents have not begun, order them to begin before the next court hearing to comply with ASFA's reasonable efforts requirements. When reunification is planned, ask whether the parents' mental health needs are being successfully addressed as part of the case plan.

When evaluating the ability of parents struggling with mental illness to safely parent their young children, ask the following questions and refer to *A Judicial Checklist for Children and Youth Exposed to Violence*:[38]

- Does the parent demonstrate poor reality testing (a person's ability to differentiate between the external and internal worlds) or worrisome patterns of denial?
- Does the parent have a mental illness, including a character disorder, such that the capacity to nurture is severely impaired?
- If there is a psychotic diagnosis: what is the need for treatment, the ability to benefit from treatment, and the effect of medication?
- Is the parent willing to be treated?
- If the parent has a mental illness, is this worsened by close contact with the infant or by demands to meet parental responsibilities (e.g., delusional thinking centering on the infant)?
- If the parent has a history of psychosis, is the infant at the center of the parent's delusional thinking or do the infant's needs trigger difficulty for the parent?[39]

Family Violence

Parents facing personal violence (or the threat of it) from an intimate partner are often distracted from caring appropriately for their young children. They have low self-esteem and tend to suffer from depression. Researchers estimate that as many as 75% of the parents who abuse or neglect their children were themselves maltreated in childhood.[40] Their experiences as children impair their ability to appropriately care for their own young children because they never learned to form healthy attachments. Child-parent psychotherapy, discussed later in this chapter, attempts to uncover the parent's own childhood trauma as the therapist works with both parent and child to broker a mutually enjoyable relationship.

When domestic violence is a factor in the child protection case,[41] case plans must address the unique needs of each family member, including the batterer and the adult and child victims.[42] In determining placement, respect the autonomy of the nonoffending parent and support her ability to provide a safe and nurturing home for the children.[43] Batterers must be held accountable for their actions. They should have a separate case plan that requires them to stop all forms of abuse toward any family member, abide by all court orders, and participate in counseling and educational programs designed for domestic batterers.[44]

Low Cognitive Functioning

Parents with low IQs face challenges caring for their children. If their intelligence is too compromised, they may not be capable of understanding and supporting their children's needs.[45] They also may not receive the support they need themselves to parent effectively. In assessing a parent's ability to care for an infant, questions about their ability to provide responsive caregiving help determine their ability to support their infant's mental health. An important consideration for parents with diminished cognitive functioning is FASD, the single greatest cause of nongenetic mental retardation. The IQ deficit is compounded by other neurological deficits that impair the victims' ability to follow directions or learn from their mistakes.[46] Proper diagnosis can lead to developing a case plan for the parent and child that permits them to live safely together.

Poverty

Poverty is the single most important predictor of neglect.[47] Living in poverty adds tremendous stress and interferes with the parents' ability to care for their young children. Poverty puts mothers at high risk for depression, post traumatic stress disorder, and for difficulties establishing nurturing relationships with their very young children.[48] Among these mothers' greatest challenges are creating a safe environment, and providing food and a place to live for themselves and their children.

Order a determination of the intensity and type of services required to meet the family's needs.

Case plans should refer parents to parenting programs that have been evaluated and found effective. Whenever possible, programs that target parents' special needs should be used. Programs exist for parents with substance abuse issues, parents of young children, and fathers. Avoid parenting classes taught by instructors who lecture parents about parenting. Rather, seek programs that allow

Incredible Years and the Strengthening Families Program

The following two programs meet established criteria for effectiveness in helping families address their special needs:

▶ **Incredible Years** offers training to help parents and teachers intervene in children's conduct problems when they are very young and develop their social competence. Curricula are available that address children in the general population, children experiencing behavior problems, and children with mental health diagnoses like attention deficit hyperactivity disorder. The experience of the teachers is related to the intensity of the intervention (e.g., therapists and teachers offer the curriculum for children with mental health diagnoses).

▶ **The Strengthening Families Program** was developed for families at risk for maltreatment. The program has developed specialized curricula for families with various cultural backgrounds (e.g., Asian and Pacific Islanders, American Indians). Like the Incredible Years, their curricula are specific to children of various ages, including a curriculum for parents and their three-to-five year olds. Although they do not yet have a curriculum for babies and toddlers, it is a model worth considering because of its curricula in Spanish, with cultural sensitivity for a wide range of ethnically diverse populations, and its extensive use with families dealing with child maltreatment.

Source: Substance Abuse and Mental Health Services Administration. National Registry of Evidence-Based Programs and Practices, 2008. Available at www.nationalregistry.samhsa.gov/submit.htm.

parents to practice new skills. The Substance Abuse and Mental Health Services Administration (SAMHSA) in the U.S. Department of Health and Human Services has established a national registry of research-based parenting interventions that may or may not target parents with substance abuse issues (www.nationalregistry.samhsa.gov/index.htm). Programs must show, at a minimum, that:

- they achieve positive outcomes in mental health and/or substance use behavior among individuals, communities, or populations;
- proven program results are documented in a peer-reviewed publication or a comprehensive evaluation report;
- guidance on implementing the program (e.g., manuals, process guides, tools, training materials) is available to the public to aid dissemination.[49]

Among programs listed are the Incredible Years and the Strengthening Families Program. Several others with an established research base have requested review by the national registry. These include Child-Parent Psychotherapy and the Nurturing Parenting Program. Each intervention focuses on special populations (e.g., families with substance abuse issues, young children).

Effective programs share certain characteristics:[50] (1) regular in-class opportunities for the parent and child to practice the information they are receiving; and (2) assessments of the parent's skills and emotional relationship with the child before the classes begin and again at the end.

Order an assessment to determine whether the child and parent would benefit from Child-Parent Psychotherapy.[51]

This intervention focuses jointly on the parent and infant. Child-Parent Psychotherapy (CPP) for mothers, fathers, and their infants and toddlers (birth to three) helps the parent read, interpret, and respond to the infant's cues. A therapist serves as a guide for the parent, helping her understand what the baby might be feeling and how the parent's needs might influence her responses to the baby.[52] Roleplaying with the infant also allows the parent to uncover traumatic experiences from his own childhood and to look at interactions from the young child's point of view.[53]

Parents also receive concrete assistance, such as transportation to appointments or a school function of an older sibling. The therapist helps with life problems such as housing that interfere with the parent's ability to focus on the clinical aspect of CPP. The therapist's positive regard for the parent in these very tangible ways helps the parent heal negative experiences with attachment figures from his or her own childhood.

Positive outcomes for those who complete CPP include:
- improved perceptions of the baby by the parent;
- improved socioemotional functioning;
- stronger parent-child relationship;
- secure attachment between parent and child; and
- improved mental health of parent.[54]

Order an assessment of whether the child and parent would benefit from Parent-Child Interaction Therapy (PCIT).[55]

This therapy was designed for two-to-six year olds with disruptive behavioral characteristics of oppositional-defiant or conduct disorder, and children with insecure attachment. It is a short-term intervention (10 to 16 weekly sessions). At first it emphasizes improving the parent-child relationship. Once certain therapeutic goals are reached, the emphasis shifts to implementing consistent discipline with the child.

PCIT is effective except when the mother is highly critical or severely depressed or when the parents are abusing drugs, experiencing severe marital discord or psychopathology.[56] Some evidence suggests that the family's relationship with the therapist is more predictive of treatment outcome than any specific therapeutic techniques. While concrete assistance with life tasks is not part of the therapeutic design, "Prinz and Miller (1994) found that families whose treatment focused exclusively on parent training and child behavior dropped out more often than families who had opportunities to discuss life concerns beyond child management, particularly among families facing greater adversity."[57]

Ensure services respond to the needs of different ethnic and cultural groups.

Little data describes effective mental health interventions for children who are not white and middle class. Ethnic minorities are less likely to begin a mental health intervention or complete treatment once therapy has begun. Practical considerations make it difficult for these families to attend regular sessions (e.g., transportation, cost). Beyond these practical barriers to participation, ethnic minority families often do not perceive services as culturally appropriate for them.[58] Case management, like that provided in CPP, is an important way to help poor and ethnic minority families meet very basic needs like housing and sufficient food.[59]

Some ethnic and cultural groups often have beliefs about child rearing that do not conform to mainstream expectations. Extended family, broadly defined to include people with whom the child has a family-like relationship, play an important role in many cultures.[60] In some cultures the autonomy that is promoted among young middle class white American children is not encouraged; rather children are encouraged to conform to standards established by adults.[61]

In cases involving Native American families, make sure the provisions of the Indian Child Welfare Act are followed. In every case you can ask parents if they feel they have been treated with respect. Ask attorneys and caseworkers to bring cultural factors to the court's attention, such as a family's reluctance to seek a blood transfusion for a severely anemic child. To enhance your ability to respond appropriately to diverse families, organize or participate in judicial training in cultural competence that addresses the diverse cultures represented in your jurisdiction.

Early Care and Education

Ensure children participate in positive early childhood learning experiences.

Early childhood is a time of intense growth and development in all areas, including rapid changes in motor development, cognition, and emotions.[62] All young children need positive early learning experiences to foster their intellectual, social, and emotional development and to lay the foundation for later school success. Infants and toddlers who have been abused or neglected need additional supports to promote their healthy growth and development and overcome adverse outcomes.

Early care and education encompasses nursery schools, prekindergarten programs, family child care homes, preschools, Head Start and Early Head Start, and care provided by families, friends, and neighbors. Care providers include private nonprofit agencies, for-profit companies, faith-based organizations, public schools, and in-home providers.

Early care and education programs and services are used in the child welfare setting for:

- an enrichment experience for the child;
- child care so foster parents or relative caregivers can work outside the home;
- respite care to allow caregivers time away from the children to care for themselves (e.g., when a parent has mental or physical illness issues that need to be addressed);
- oversight to allow the court or child welfare agency to watch for maltreatment in the home (biological or substitute caregiver's);
- a neutral professional setting for visitation with parent coaching;
- an opportunity for the child to be involved in consistent peer relationships and receive sensory and cognitive support that might not be available at home.

Referrals or court orders specifying early care and education programs should weigh the potential benefits and drawbacks.

Benefits:

- **Early relationships.** Early childhood education programs that promote small groups, continuity of caregivers, and individualized care can help young children who have been abused and neglected develop essential early relationships that are associated with adaptive social development.[63]

- **Caregiver support.** High-quality early care and education programs can also support foster, kinship, and biological parents by directing them to other support systems, providing information, and connecting them with other parents who can offer advice and support.[64] Comprehensive early childhood programs like Early Head Start combine home visitation and comprehensive center-based services that also provide opportunities for the parent to learn and model supportive parenting strategies.

- **Specialized services for children.** Early care and education programs can provide the specialized services that very young children in the child welfare system need, including opportunities for enhanced social-emotional health and development. In addition, therapeutic child care programs that address issues faced by abused and neglected children can ensure that these young children are receiving specialized treatment and attention.

Drawbacks:

- **Staff training.** Child care is only as good as the teachers who staff the program.[65] If staff has not received adequate training, children under their care will not receive the quality experiences that promote their healthy development.

- **Quality.** While there has been no definitive study of the quality of care available for infants and toddlers, research shows that much available care is not optimal.[66] Placing a very young child in a low or poor quality child care situation may cause further harm to a child already suffering from developmental or mental health issues as a result of abuse or neglect.

- **Staff turnover.** Even the best programs struggle with staff turnover due to very low wages. High rates of staff turnover—nearly 40% per year, nationally —mean that the warm, caring relationship between a child and teacher is frequently disrupted. The result is poor quality care and children who show lower language and social skills.[67] This instability prevents babies and toddlers from developing secure attachments to their child care providers.[68]

Carefully consider the availability and quality of early care and education settings.

Consider the following factors when deciding to place a child in an early care and education setting:

- **Can the foster parent stay home with the child?** This is typically a better option for very young children if the foster parent provides nurturing, developmentally appropriate care. Opportunities for enriched learning experiences can be sought through facilitated play groups, museum programs, and in-home services for developmentally delayed children. The foster parent should receive training in developmental milestones and in appropriate ways to engage young children from birth and beyond so they can enrich the home environment.

- **If not, what type of program would best meet the child's needs?** Early Head Start focuses on the child in the context of his family and works to involve families. Traditional child care programs may play no role in families' lives beyond providing care for the child each day. Care provided by a neighbor may give the foster parent flexibility and provide the child with individualized care, assuming the quality of the neighbor's care is closely examined and verified (e.g., proper licensing, training, and experience).

- **How many hours per day and days per week should the child attend?** Limiting the number of hours away from the child's primary caregiver will make the transition easier for the child within a regular schedule (e.g., Monday, Wednesday, and Friday from 9:00 until 12:00).

- **Will the child be assigned to one specific primary teacher who is present most of the child's day in care?** Expanding the circle of primary caregivers to include one teacher in a safe and engaging learning environment is positive for maltreated children. Less than this level of personalized attention has the potential to add to the child's existing confusion and sense of powerlessness.

- **Does the program provide in-home services where the child and parent receive individual attention and guidance?** This training helps parents apply loving strategies to their relationships with their children.

- **Can the child care program be used as a location for visits between noncustodial parents and their young children?** Holding visits in a familiar setting makes the experience less stressful for the child. Depending how child care staff handles the visits, parent and child can engage in supported interactions and classroom activities that will strengthen their relationship and better equip the parent to care for the child.

- **Who pays for the care?** Some of the most significant issues regarding early care and education relate to access and capacity of the programs to enroll children. For example, Early Head Start is a federal entitlement program. Families whose incomes fall below the federal definition of poverty are eligible to enroll. However, due to limited funding only 3%

of eligible infants and toddlers are able to participate.[69] Public preschool programs are part-day programs that are typically offered free to children living in the school's community. Some states grant eligibility for state subsidized child care when children come into contact with the child welfare system. State child care subsidy programs are administered by multiple agencies across the 50 states. Eligibility requirements differ as do state funds available to support children in care.

Conclusion

During infancy and early childhood, the child's brain develops its capacity for trust, self-esteem, conscience, empathy, problem solving, focused learning, and self control.[70] While research continues to reveal what a child needs for healthy development throughout this period, much is already known:[71]

- All children have the capacity to learn and experience feelings from birth.
- Creating nurturing and secure early environments is essential to healthy development.
- Parental health and well-being affects children's development.
- Early and focused interventions can increase the chances of positive developmental outcomes when early childhood is disrupted.

Well-conceived interventions can minimize or even reverse the effects of damaging early childhood experiences. By arming yourself with the science of early childhood and learning about effective interventions, you can improve the outcomes for the children under your court's jurisdiction.

Endnotes

1. Perry, B.D. "Childhood Experience and the Expression of Genetic Potential: What Childhood Neglect Tells Us about Nature and Nurture." *Brain and Mind* 3, 2002, 79-100.

2. Foulds, B. et al. *Infant Toddler Module 1: Social Emotional Development with the Context of Relationships*. Washington, DC: Center on the Social and Emotional Foundations for Early Learning, 2008.

3. The field of attachment research began with the work of British psychoanalyst John Bowlby. Mary Ainsworth tested and corroborated Dr. Bowlby's theory through "strange situation" experiments where very young children and their parents were observed at separation and reunion and during the introduction of a stranger. Dr. Ainsworth documented the quality of the attachment between young children and their parents in multiple settings in the U.S. and abroad. She identified three types of attachment. Years later a student of Dr. Ainsworth's, Mary Main, identified a fourth category.

4. Karen, R. *Becoming Attached: First Relationships and How They Shape Our Capacity to Love*. New York: Oxford University Press, 1994.

5. Tartar, R.E. "Etiology of Adolescent Substance Abuse: A Developmental Perspective."

American Journal of Addiction 11(3), 2002, 171-91. Available at www.ncbi.nlm.nih.gov/pubmed/ 12202010?ordinalpos=33&itool=EntrezSystem2.PEntrez.Pubmed.Pubmed_ResultsPanel.Pubmed _DefaultReportPanel.Pubmed_RVDocSum; Whitbeck, L.B. and D.R. Hoyt. *Nowhere to Grow: Homeless and Runaway Adolescents and Their Families.* New York: Aldine de Gruyter, 1999; Irving, B. and C. Bloxcom. *Predicting Adolescent Delinquent Behavior and Criminal Conviction by Age 30; Evidence from the British Birth Cohort.* London, England: Police Foundation, 2002.

6. Infant mental health disorders are defined as emotional and behavioral patterns that interfere significantly with very young children's capacity to meet age-appropriate, cultural, and community expectations for managing emotions, forming close and secure interpersonal relationships, and exploring the environment. Zeanah, C.H., ed. *Handbook of Infant Mental Health,* 2d ed. New York: Guilford, 1999; U.S. Department of Health and Human Services. *Pathways to Prevention: A Comprehensive Guide for Supporting Infant and Toddler Mental Health,* 2004.

7. Diamond-Berry, K. and L. Hudson. *Intergenerational Chemical Addiction: Improving Outcomes for Maltreated Infants, Toddlers, and Their Families.* Washington, DC: American Bar Association Center on Children and the Law & Zero to Three Policy Center, in press.

8. Lieberman, A.F. et al. "Violence in Infancy and Early Childhood: Relationship-Based Treatment and Evaluation." *Interventions for Children Exposed to Violence.* Edited by A.F. Lieberman and R. DeMartino. New Brunswick, NJ: Johnson & Johnson Pediatric Institute, 2006, 65-83.

9. Ibid.

10. Siegel, D. "The Mindful Brain: Healing in the Face of Trauma." A Conference on Childhood Trauma: Integrating Research and Practice. Mentor, OH: Crossroads, Lake County Alcohol, Drug Addiction and Mental Health Services Board, 2008.

11. "AACAP/CWLA Policy Statement on Mental Health and Use of Alcohol and Other Drugs, Screening and Assessment of Children in Foster Care." American Academy of Child and Adolescent Psychiatry, 2003. Available at www.aacap.org/cs/root/policy_statements/aacap/ cwla_policy_statement_on_mental_health_and_use_of_alcohol_and_other_drugs_screening_ and_assessment_of_children_in_foster_care.

12. American Academy of Pediatrics, Council on Children With Disabilities. "Identifying Infants and Young Children with Developmental Disorders in the Medical Home: An Algorithm for Developmental Surveillance and Screening." *Pediatrics* 118, 2006, 405-420.

13. Infant & Toddler Coordinators Association. *Infant Mental Health Approaches and IDEA Part C.* Indianapolis, IN: Infant & Toddler Coordinators Association, 2005. Available at www.ideainfanttoddler.org/ITCA_infant_Mental_Health_7_05.pdf.

14. Ibid., 7.

15. Ibid., 6.

16. Jones Harden, B. *Infants in the Child Welfare System: A Developmental Framework for Policy and Practice.* Washington, DC: Zero to Three, 2007, 169-184.

17. AACAP/CWLA Policy Statement, 2003.

18. Ibid.

19. This section includes excerpts from Smariga, M. *Visitation with Infants and Toddlers in Foster Care: What Judges and Attorneys Need to Know.* Washington, DC: American Bar Association Center on Children and the Law & Zero to Three Policy Center, 2007.

20. Goldsmith, D.F., D. Oppenheim and J. Wanlass. "Separation and Reunification: Using Attachment Theory and Research to Inform Decisions Affecting the Placements of Children in Foster Care." *Juvenile and Family Court Journal* 55(2), 2004, 1–13.

21. American Academy of Pediatrics Committee on Early Childhood, Adoption and Dependent Care. "Developmental Issues for Young Children in Foster Care." *Pediatrics* 105(5), 2000, 1146.

22. American Academy of Pediatrics, Committee on Early Childhood, Adoption, and Dependent Care. "Developmental Issues for Young Children in Foster Care." (Policy Statement) *Pediatrics* 106(5), 2000, 1145-1150.

23. Ginther, N.M. and J.D. Ginther. "Family Interaction: The Expressway to Permanency— Facilitating Successful Visitation." Presentation prepared for Western Training Partnership at the University of Wisconsin River Falls, 2005, 12-13.

24. Ohio Caseload Analysis Initiative. *Visitation/Family Access Guide: A Best Practice Model for Social Workers and Agencies*, 2005, 14.

25. Ginther and Ginther, 2005, 10, 21.

26. Wright, Lois E. *Toolbox No. 1: Using Visitation to Support Permanency.* Washington, DC: CWLA Press, 2001; Ohio Caseload Analysis Initiative, 2005, 16.

27. Wright, 2001; Ohio Caseload Analysis Initiative, 2005.

28. Goldsmith et al., 2004, 2; Wright, 2001, 28–32.

29. Wright, 2001, 23–28; Haight, W.L. et al. "Making Visits Better: The Perspectives of Parents, Foster Parents, and Child Welfare Workers." *Child Welfare* 81(2), 2002, 173–202.

30. P.L. 110-351.

31. Committee on Integrating the Science of Early Childhood Development, National Research Council and Institute of Medicine. *From Neurons to Neighborhoods: The Science of Early Childhood Development.* Edited by Shonkoff, J.P and D.A. Phillips. Board on Children, Youth, and Families, Commission on Behavioral and Social Sciences and Education. Washington, DC: National Academy Press, 2000, 390.

32. Schuder, M.R. and K. Lyons-Ruth. "'Hidden Trauma' in Infancy: Attachment, Fearful Arousal, and Early Dysfunction of the Stress Response System." In *Young Children and Trauma: Intervention and Treatment.* Edited by J.D. Osofsky. New York: Guilford Press, 2004, 70.

33. Jones Harden, B., 2007, 56-57.

34. Boger, R.P. and A.B. Smith. "Developing Parental Skills: An Holistic, Longitudinal Process." *Infant Mental Health Journal* 7(2), 2006, 7.

35. Jones Harden, B., 2007, 46.

36. Jones Harden, B., 2007, 187.

37. Onunaku, N. *Improving Maternal and Infant Mental Health: Focus on Maternal Depression.* Los Angeles, CA: National Center for Infant and Early Childhood Health Policy, 2004, 4.

38. Office of Juvenile Justice and Delinquency Prevention. *A Judicial Checklist for Children and Youth Exposed to Violence.* Reno, NV: National Council of Juvenile and Family Court Judges, 2006. Available at www.safestartcenter.org/pdf/childandyouth_tabrief.pdf.

39. Boger and Smith, 2006, 26.

40. Larrieu, J.A. and S.M. Bellow. "Relationship Assessment for Young Traumatized Children." In *Young Children and Trauma: Intervention and Treatment.* Edited by J.D. Osofsky. New York: Guilford Press, 2004, 156.

41. Edwards, L. *Domestic Violence and the Child Protection Court.* Reno: NV: National Council of Juvenile and Family Court Judges, The Greenbook Initiative. Available at http://thegreenbook.info/documents/l_edwards_col.pdf.

42. Fitzgerald, R. "Reasonable Efforts Determinations in Co-Occurrence Cases: A Policy Discussion." *2003 Judges' Toolbox Meeting Executive Summary.* Reno, NV: National Council of Juvenile and Family Court Judges, The Greenbook Initiative, 2003. Available at www.thegreenbook.info/documents/JT_Exec_Summ.pdf.

43. Ibid.

44. Schechter, S. and J.L. Edleson et al. *Effective Intervention in Domestic Violence & Child Maltreatment Cases: Guidelines for Policy and Practice, Recommendations from the National Council of Juvenile and Family Court Judges.* Reno, NV: National Council of Juvenile and Family Court Judges, 1998.

45. Jones Harden, B., 2007, 186.

46. Hudson, Lucy, Larry Burd and Kay Kelly. *Recognizing Fetal Alcohol Spectrum Disorder (FASD) in Maltreated Infants and Toddlers and Their Parents*. Washington, DC: American Bar Association Center on Children and the Law & Zero to Three Policy Center, in press.

47. Jones Harden, B., 2007, 57.

48. Committee on Integrating the Science of Early Childhood Development, National Research Council and Institute of Medicine, 2000, 353.

49. Substance Abuse and Mental Health Services Administration. "Submissions." *National Registry of Evidence-Based Programs and Practices*, 2008. Available at www.nationalregistry. samhsa.gov/submit.htm.

50. Katz, L. "Parenting Classes: The Good, The Bad, and the Ugly." Presentation to Zero to Three Court Teams for Maltreated Infants and Toddlers Project Staff and Consultants, 2007.

51. Lieberman, A.F., R. Silverman and J.H. Pawl. "Infant-Parent Psychotherapy." In *Handbook of Infant Mental Health*, 2d ed. Edited by C.H. Zeanah, Jr. New York: Guilford Press, 2000, 432.

52. Carter, S.L., J.D. Osofsky and D.M. Hann. "Speaking for Baby: Therapeutic Intervention with Adolescent Mothers and Their Infants." *Infant Mental Health Journal* 12(4), 1991, 291-302.

53. University of Miami Linda Ray Intervention Center, Eleventh Judicial Circuit of Florida. *Miami Safe Start Initiative Replication Manual*, 2005, 14-15.

54. Lieberman, A.F. et al., 2006, 76-79.

55. Herschell, A.D. et al. "Parent-Child Interaction Therapy: New Directions in Research." *Cognitive and Behavioral Practice* 9, 2002, 9-16.

56. Ibid.

57. Ibid.

58. Lewis, M.L. and C.G. Ippen. "Rainbows of Tears, Souls Full of Hope: Cultural Issues Related to Young Children and Trauma." In *Young Children and Trauma: Intervention and Treatment*. Edited by J.D. Osofsky. New York: Guilford Press, 2004, 11-16.

59. Ibid., 33.

60. Ibid., 28.

61. Ibid., 30.

62. Committee on Integrating the Science of Early Childhood Development, National Research Council and Institute of Medicine, 2000.

63. Ibid., 309.

64. Dicker, S., E. Gordon and J. Knitzer. *Improving the Odds for the Healthy Development of Young Children in Foster Care*. New York: National Center for Children in Poverty, 2001.

65. Shonkoff and Phillips, 2000, 310.

66. See generally Vandell, D.L. and B. Wolfe. *Child Care Quality: Does It Matter and Does It Need to be Improved?* Madison, WI: Institute for Research on Poverty, University of Wisconsin-Madison, 2000. Available at http://aspe.hhs.gov/hsp/ccquality00/ccqual.htm#1.

67. National Association for the Education of Young Children. "Where Your Child Care Dollars Go." Washington, DC: National Association for the Education of Young Children, 2008. Available at www.naeyc.org/ece/1997/07.asp.

68. Committee on Integrating the Science of Early Childhood Development, National Research Council and Institute of Medicine, 2000, 235.

69. Schumacher, R. and L. DeLauro. *Building on the Promise: State Initiatives to Expand Access to Early Head Start for Young Children and Their Families*. Washington, DC: Center for Law and Social Policy/Zero to Three, 2008, 7.

70. American Academy of Pediatrics, Committee on Early Childhood, Adoption, and Dependent Care. "Health Care of Young Children in Foster Care" (Policy Statement). *Pediatrics* 109(3), 2002, 536-541.

71. Shonkoff and Phillips, 2000.

Achieving Permanency

Achieving Permanency

Timely Permanency and Healthy Child Development
▶ Plan for permanency from day one.
▶ Consider the rapid and multifaceted development of a very young child when determining permanency goals.

Preliminary Protective Hearings
▶ Determine the relative harm of nonremoval versus the potential psychological harm of removal.
▶ Determine if the child-placing agency has made reasonable efforts to prevent removal.
▶ If the child will be removed, identify appropriate caregivers.
▶ Seek the least disruptive, most family-like setting.
▶ Evaluate child care/early education options for the child.
▶ Devise a plan for parent-child and sibling contact.
▶ Request the child's medical records and order screening to identify the child's health needs.
▶ Identify services for the parent.

Disposition and Case Planning
▶ If a placement change is needed, identify the safest, most family-like placement.
▶ Revisit reunification.
▶ Identify the child's needs and available family resources.
▶ Assess caregiver supports.
▶ Require comprehensive individualized case planning in each case.
▶ Encourage family group conferencing.
▶ Ensure concurrent planning begins early in the case.
▶ Identify the family's service needs.
▶ Ensure a comprehensive visitation plan is developed.

Review Hearings
▶ Assess whether the issues that caused the child's removal are being addressed.
▶ Order additional services or reassessments for the child.
▶ Evaluate safety and risk factors if the child will return home.

▶ Determine if the substitute caregiver supports the parent toward reunification.

▶ Assess the visitation plan and whether changes are needed.

Permanency Hearings

▶ Determine if reunification is a viable permanency plan.

▶ Identify how reunification will affect the child in the short term.

▶ Ensure transition planning is part of a reunification plan.

▶ Determine if adoption is a viable permanency plan.

▶ Determine if the current caregiver can adopt the child.

▶ Consider ordering mediation to resolve adoption-related concerns.

▶ Determine if legal guardianship is a viable permanency plan.

▶ Determine if relative placement is a viable permanency plan, only after exploring more desirable options.

▶ In most cases, APPLA should not be a permanency goal for very young children.

▶ Hear the child's views regarding the permanency plan.

▶ Observe preverbal children in court to inform your decision making.

▶ Consider the child's developmental stage during courtroom observations.

▶ Determine if there is cause to extend the goal of reunification.

Postpermanency Support for Young Children and Their Families

▶ Ensure supports are in place to sustain reunification.

▶ Identify adoption disruption factors.

▶ Identify postadoption supports.

▶ Ensure postadoption supports and services are equally available to permanent guardians or long-term relative caregivers.

▶ Maintain family connections.

Very young children in the child welfare system require stable and nurturing caregivers and environments to encourage their healthy development. As the judge, you can promote permanency and healthy development for these children by ordering placement, services, and visitation arrangements that support their primary attachments and relationships.

Research reveals that very young children, especially infants, enter care in greater numbers than older children. Very young children are less likely to reunify with their parents, are more likely to be adopted, and experience longer stays in care.[1] Moreover, very young children reenter the child welfare system after reunification in higher numbers, especially within the first 90 days.[2]

Your leadership from the bench is essential to:

- achieve timely permanency,
- decrease foster care reentries, and
- enhance overall well-being outcomes for very young children in the child welfare system.

Timely Permanency and Healthy Child Development

The Adoption and Safe Families Act of 1997 (ASFA)[3] shortens the timeframes for making permanency decisions for children in foster care. It also requires termination of parental rights proceedings for those children in foster care for 15 out of 22 months and includes special protections for abandoned infants. Permanency is a focal point, requiring heightened reviews by judges and less opportunity for foster care drift. ASFA's push for timely permanency responds to the very young child's sense of time—especially for infants under one year old—by supporting key attachments and relationships during early child development. ASFA's requirement to advance the multiple goals of permanency, child safety, and child well-being is best approached by focusing on the child's specific developmental and emotional needs.[4]

ASFA emphasizes child well-being and the Child and Family Services Review (CFSR) measures states' performance in this area.[5] This focus on well-being is critical for very young children in the child welfare system. You can meet ASFA's requirements by using the court process to ensure early intervention and infant mental health services are provided that promote child well-being and timely permanency from the onset of the case.

Resources on Cultural Competence

Cultural competence within the dependency court allows judges, attorneys, court personnel, social workers and other stakeholders to work effectively with people from different cultures to improve decision-making and services designed to meet the needs of children and families. The cultural context of a case is more than race and ethnicity, but also includes economic status, education level, gender, age, sexual orientation, language, immigration status, disabilities, and many more factors. Cultural competence enables individuals to expand the scope of what they view as relevant facts to include the total life experiences of the children and families before the court.

Resources that can help you consider culture when making decisions for children and families include:

▸ **Courts Catalyzing Change: Achieving Equity and Fairness in Foster Care**
www.ncjfcj.org/content/blogcategory/447/580/
The National Council of Juvenile and Family Court Judges' Courts Catalyzing Change Initiative brought together judicial officers and other systems' experts and set a national agenda for court-based training, research, and reform initiatives to reduce the disproportionate representation of children of color in dependency court systems.

▸ **National Center for Cultural Competence**
www11.georgetown.edu/research/gucchd/nccc/
The National Center for Cultural Competence at the Georgetown University Center for Child and Human Development seeks to increase the capacity of health care and mental health care programs to design, implement, and evaluate culturally and linguistically competent service delivery systems to address growing diversity, persistent disparities, and to promote health and mental health equity.

▸ **Child Welfare Information Gateway: Cultural Competence**
www.childwelfare.gov/systemwide/cultural/
This site offers resources to help professionals in the child welfare system better understand and enhance their cultural competence. It provides information on working with children, youth, and families; disproportional representation of minority groups in the child welfare system; culturally competent services; training for child welfare staff; and the specific role of cultural competence in child maltreatment, out-of-home care, and adoption.

▸ *Making Differences Work* **(ABA Center on Children and the Law, 1996)**
www.abanet.org/abastore/ (Search product code 5490051)
This book by Karen Aileen Howze seeks to help attorneys and judges question the assumptions and perceptions that play an important role in how determinations about the best interests of children in the dependency court are made.

Plan for permanency from day one.

When determining permanency goals and approaches, consider the rapid and multifaceted development of a very young child discussed in Chapters 2 and 3, as well as the prevailing research about permanency outcomes and length of time in care for very young children. Your decisions at key points and hearings during the child's time in care are essential to promoting positive permanent outcomes that consider the very young child's cognitive, physical, and social-emotional development, and well-being.

The National Council of Juvenile and Family Court Judges' *RESOURCE GUIDELINES: Improving Court Practice in Child Abuse & Neglect Cases*[6] (*RESOURCE GUIDELINES*) identify key decisions and questions that judges should focus on at each stage of the court process. The following discussion about permanency for very young children looks at these and other key decisions and how they affect infants, toddlers, and preschoolers involved with the dependency court process.[7]

Preliminary Protective Hearings

Key decisions and questions for the judge:[8]

- ▸ Should the child return home immediately?
- ▸ What services will allow the child to remain safely at home?
- ▸ Will the parties voluntarily agree to participate in such services?
- ▸ Has the agency made reasonable efforts to avoid protective placement of the child?
- ▸ Are responsible relatives or other adults available?
- ▸ Is the placement proposed by the agency the least disruptive and most family-like setting that meets the needs of the child?
- ▸ Is the child placed with adults who could become the child's permanent caregivers if reunification efforts fail?
- ▸ Will the service plan and the child's continued well-being be monitored on an ongoing basis by a guardian ad litem (GAL) or court appointed special advocate (CASA)?
- ▸ Are restraining orders, or orders expelling an allegedly abusive parent from the home appropriate?
- ▸ Are orders needed for examinations, evaluations, or immediate services?
- ▸ What are the terms and conditions for parental visitation or family time?
- ▸ What are the financial support needs of the child?

Removal & Placement

Determine the relative harm of nonremoval versus the potential psychological harm of removal.

Because they are physically defenseless and in a state of rapid development, very young children are at great risk of suffering harm from maltreatment. Even so, removal from biological parents, even when fully justified and necessary, forever alters a young child's life.[9] Thus, both the maltreatment *and* the resulting removal can disrupt the very young child's development and overall well-being. When determining the need for removal, always balance safety concerns with the potential psychological and developmental harm of removal.

Determine if the child-placing agency has made reasonable efforts to prevent removal.

When removal is being recommended or has occurred, determine whether reasonable efforts to prevent the removal were made. For the very young child, these efforts should include intensive, in-home, or residential services that promote an infant's safety while allowing him to remain in the care of his parents. For families with substance abuse issues, some communities have residential drug treatment programs for mothers and their young children that support a mother's recovery and the parent-child relationship, while providing the structure and supervision to protect the child. Domestic violence shelters and transitional housing programs are often designed for a mother and her young children. These programs may have child care centers on-site or an affiliated center so mothers can work on their recovery and self-efficacy. Although less common, some jurisdictions also offer residential services for fathers and their children.[10] In these cases, the court can still take jurisdiction and closely monitor the parent's compliance with treatment and the well-being of the infant.

If the child will be removed, identify appropriate caregivers.

If reasonable efforts have been made to prevent removal or if a child's safety requires removal, finding an appropriate caregiver is essential. Whether a relative, nonrelative, or licensed foster parent, the caregiver must be physically and emotionally prepared to care for the special needs of an infant.

Ensuring Substitute Care Meets the Needs of Infants

Infants who enter foster care are vulnerable due to the maltreatment and trauma they have experienced. The type of substitute care in which they are placed, often for long periods, creates added risks when the caregivers are physically, psychologically, or financially unprepared to provide quality care. Kinship caregivers have high levels of psychosocial challenges such as stress, depression or trauma, and may face greater problems than nonrelative foster parents.

Opportunities exist to enhance the skills and understanding of caregivers and tailor caregiving environments to each infant's needs. This approach emphasizes promoting infant development through their relationships with their caregivers. Even when those caregivers are temporary, they can positively or negatively affect the infant's development.

Family foster parents and kinship caregivers should:

▶ Understand infant and child development and the infant's developmental needs.

▶ Develop infant-centered home environments.

▶ Partner with the child welfare agency by participating in planning meetings and advocating for the infant's needs.

▶ Empathize with infant experiences, past and present, and understand that infants remember and respond to memories of past trauma.

▶ Respect, honor, and support the multiple familial connections that infants have to their parents, former foster parents, and others. Acknowledge that these connections may affect their ability to attach to new caregivers (especially if the infant has endured multiple moves).

▶ Be willing to reflect on their attitudes and behaviors about children and be open to developing new skills and challenging previous assumptions and beliefs.

▶ Be flexible enough to adapt to an infant's irregular eating and sleeping schedules and be physically capable of lifting, carrying, feeding, diapering and bathing an infant.

▶ Be able to handle *dysregulated* infants (excessive crying and feeding challenges, typical of maltreated infants) and be able to respond when the infant is in need.

▶ Be willing to play with the infant and follow her lead and nonverbal cues.

▶ Be supportive of the infant's placement in a permanent home.

▶ Take advantage of available resources to support placement.

Child welfare agencies should:

▶ Provide caregivers with specific infant-oriented support to ensure an infant-centered home environment (e.g., age-appropriate toys, care items, books).

▶ Engage caregivers as advocates and partner with them in seeking services and interventions through other social service systems.

▶ Develop foster parent training that teaches how to meet the multiple needs of infants in their care and addresses knowledge, attitudes, and beliefs.

▶ Select foster parents based on their ability and willingness to meet the requirements in the above list. Screenings and home studies should look carefully at their ability to care for infants.

▶ Provide intervention programs to support the caregiver-infant relationship when they experience challenges, rather than instantly moving the infant to another foster home.

▶ Provide ongoing caregiver education programs that address parenting infants, with special attention to supporting maltreated or traumatized infants and creating developmentally appropriate environments for each child in their home.

▶ Clearly assess the substitute caregiver's ability to support reunification or become an adoptive parent or permanent guardian if reunification becomes untenable.

▶ Support smooth and thoughtful transitions between caregivers if such transitions become necessary for the child's ultimate permanency.

Source:
Adapted from Jones Harden, Brenda. *Infants in the Child Welfare System: A Developmental Framework for Policy & Practice*. Washington, DC: Zero to Three, 2007, 223-240. This section focuses on infants, those children birth to 12 months of age. Infants four months and younger are more likely to enter foster care and stay in care longer than any other population.

On a practical level, *all caregivers of very young children* must have:
• a crib or safe bed for the child;
• a safety-proofed home—especially for infants who are crawling and walking;
• appropriate food/formula;
• infant-safe bathing and changing areas;
• appropriate clothing and diapers;
• age-appropriate toys and books; and
• ability to meet the demanding physical and emotional needs of very young children.

Caregivers for *infants* must be prepared to:
• be woken up at night;
• change many diapers;
• wash a lot of laundry; and
• tolerate long periods of crying.

Caregivers for *toddlers and preschoolers* must:
- be able to keep up with physically active and emotionally unpredictable children;
- support toddlers' language development;
- provide safe environments in which children can exercise their new skills; and
- monitor health and behavioral signs necessary to appropriately identify potential developmental delays.

Seek the least disruptive, most family-like setting.

Early in the case, a plan for the child's 24-hour care must be laid out. A typical infant in care, especially those in kinship care, will spend some of the day with relatives, child care center staff, and/or parents. Never underestimate the importance of siblings to very young children. Thus, placement arrangements that can accommodate the very young child's siblings should be sought, especially if there is an established bond and the siblings do not act in ways that harm the infant.

Shelter or group care is not recommended for infants who have been taken into care. Not only is it not *the most family-like* setting, the shelter environment is contrary to the emotional and developmental needs of very young children.

If a relative is being considered:
- Determine from the onset whether the relative:
  - knows about the needs of very young children;
  - can manage the physical demands of caring for an infant;
  - will facilitate visitation and the parent-child bonding and attachment process;
  - is aware of the parents' challenges and any limitations placed by the court;
  - is able and willing to become a permanent caregiver if the need arises.
- Ensure the relative has help obtaining the financial support (i.e., relative caregiver funds) and/or child care services they will need to meet the infant's needs.
- Explore the possibility of the relative taking in a teen parent and the infant, especially in cases in which the parent lacks parenting skills but is interested in the infant and wants to learn how to be a responsible parent.
- Ensure a home study is completed if required. Some jurisdictions require a preadoptive home study of any relative being considered to provide substitute care to a child under age three.

- Ask about the number of children in the home, their ages, and any potential risks they may pose to the infant or toddler. While having many children in a home is not necessarily a cause for concern, be sure the caregiver can care for the intensive needs of a young child on top of other obligations.

- Assess the noncustodial parent, often the father and/or the child's paternal relatives, as potential caregivers for a very young child. Involving the noncustodial parent and his/her relatives early is an important step towards ensuring future permanency.

If foster parents are being considered:

- Assess their ability to care for very young children and their potential as long-term adoptive parents.

- Find out about the number of children in the home, their ages, and any potential risks they may pose to the infant or toddler.

- Determine the foster parent's ability to provide frequent visitation to the biological parent(s).

- Get assurance from the child-placing agency that the foster parent will support and involve the biological parents, to the extent possible, in reunification efforts. Experienced foster parents can be strong parent educators if they have the right mindset towards the biological parents.

- If the parent is a youth in care, explore whether the foster caregiver will accept the youth together with her infant.

Evaluate child care/early education options for the child.

At the preliminary protective hearing, assess the quality of any proposed child care setting and early education programs. Many jurisdictions use county or state quality rating systems with Web-based access to a child care center's rating. (See Chapter 3 for more information.)

Devise a plan for parent-child and sibling contact.

Maintaining contact between very young children and their parents helps them develop attachments during the child's first year of life. While frequent contact between a child and parent may be perceived as a burden by caseworkers and foster parents, it is one of the best predictors for successfully reunifying very young children.[11] If a very young child is not placed with his or her siblings, consider sibling visits and opportunities to support the sibling bond, especially for toddlers and preschoolers who may perceive their older siblings as caregivers.

Consider requiring an immediate 'contact conference' or meeting where parents, caregivers, family members, child care providers, service providers, GALs/CASAs and case managers develop a plan for visitation and family time that spreads the supervision and transportation responsibilities among multiple individuals. This plan should also account for preexisting formal or informal visitation agreements between the child and his noncustodial parent, siblings, and relatives.

Research shows breastfeeding can enhance the bond between mother and child and has some health benefits. Nursing mothers should be encouraged to continue nursing their infants, if possible. Parent-child contact and placement arrangements should support their efforts to breastfeed, if the safety of the infant is not jeopardized. Additionally, nursing mothers who wish their infants to have breast-milk should be able to provide it to the substitute caregiver and expect it to be fed to the infant when feasible and safe unless it is not advised for medical reasons.

Request the child's medical records and order screening to identify the child's health needs.

Many infants and young children enter the child welfare system with significant medical and/or developmental delays and challenges, or such issues emerge while they are in the system. Achieving permanency requires addressing these needs early. As discussed in Chapter 3, all states have early intervention systems that identify and address developmental needs of very young children.

At the first point of contact with a very young child, order:

- records of all screenings performed at birth as well as a Part C screening for children ages zero to three (see Chapter 3 discussion of developmental screenings);
- screenings for fetal alcohol spectrum disorders and any other effects of in utero substance exposure; and
- medical and dental screenings and oral health care for the child (see Chapter 2).

Identify services for the parent.

As the *RESOURCE GUIDELINES* suggest, services to address a parent's most pressing issues should be offered from the onset of the case. Typically, substance abuse, mental illness and/or domestic violence cause the need for removal. Often, these issues co-occur, requiring intensive, sometimes residential, interventions. Once a parent is screened and engaged in treatment to address specific needs, he or she may require further skill building or support related to parenting their very young child. Parenting courses, support groups, or parent coaches/mentors can help.

Disposition and Case Planning

Key decisions and questions for the judge:[12]

▶ What is the appropriate statutory disposition of the case and long-term permanency goal for the child?

▶ Is the child placed with adults who could become his permanent caregivers?

▶ Does the agency-proposed case plan reasonably address the problems and needs of the child and parent?

▶ Has the agency made reasonable efforts to eliminate the need for placement or prevent the need for placement?

▶ What, if any, child support should be ordered?

▶ When will the case be reviewed?

Placement

If a placement change is needed, identify the safest, most family-like placement.

Ideally a very young child will remain in the same placement while in care, and beyond if reunification is not achieved. However, sometimes it is necessary to change a child's initial placement at the disposition hearing or at other points during the child's time in care. Assess why the placement is changing. Is the change for convenience or to better meet the child's needs? Could the placement be preserved if the child and/or caregiver received more support or services?

Revisit reunification.

Before moving an infant or toddler to another foster or relative placement, assess whether reunification is safe. Evaluate whether the parent is engaged in services, consistent and attentive during visitation, and capable of caring for the child's daily needs. Also assess the special needs of the child—does he have multiple treatments or therapies and/or special medical needs? Can the parent handle these needs now or does the parent need further training, support, or services? Have the safety issues and risks been significantly reduced or eliminated?

Identify the child's needs and available family resources.

Determining the best placement depends on the specific needs of the child and the family resources available. For infants, toddlers, and preschoolers, any placement in a 24-hour group setting is not appropriate.[13]

One tool for identifying family resources is *family finding*. In this intensive process, caseworkers and/or dedicated staff search for family members or family-like connections for children in foster care. This process often involves reading every paper in a child's file and performing targeted internet searches to identify relatives. Meetings between family and the children are arranged to develop family connections. Often, these family members did not know the infant existed and are willing to step forward as potential permanent caregivers or to support the biological parents. Even when placement does not take place, the contacts are critical for young children in care and may be key to maintaining connections to their family and cultural heritage and traditions.[14]

Assess caregiver supports.

Because very young children have intensive needs, substitute caregivers will need supports. Ask these questions:

- Does the caregiver need time away from the child and respite care?
- If available, have relative caregiver funds been applied for?
- Is the infant receiving all entitlements for which she is eligible?
- Are parents providing financial assistance or support in other ways (e.g., purchasing diapers, infant care products, furniture, and clothing)?
- Is child care needed and/or established?

These supports help maintain a very young child's placement and enhance her ability to form healthy attachments, feel safe, and receive consistent and positive care.

Case Planning

Require comprehensive individualized case planning in each case.

Effective case planning achieves positive outcomes for all children in the child welfare system, especially very young children who are likely to have long stays in care. The more comprehensive and inclusive the case planning, the more likely the plan will address the family's deficits and improve its strengths.[15] For parents of very young children in care, many of whom are just becoming adults themselves, full engagement in the process is essential to achieving reunification. Assessments and screenings should be the starting point for what a child and family need, but the case plan embodies the family's strengths, behaviors, needs, conditions and contributing factors.

Encourage family group conferencing.[16]

Family group conferencing (FGC) or another structured process often aids successful reunification and speeds permanency for very young, vulnerable children. FGC brings together extended family, friends, and others to help the parents develop a plan to protect children and strengthen their caregiving abilities.

Benefits of FGC include:

- increased parent motivation and buy-in to the service planning and implementation process;
- more stable placements;
- improved case-processing times;[17]
- fewer children living in out-of-home care; and
- increased kinship placements.

Although special skills and efforts to engage the family and community are required for effective FGCs, the investment in training and expertise often speeds permanency outcomes for very young children.[18]

Ensure concurrent planning begins early in the case.

ASFA encourages concurrent case planning in permanency planning practice. Originally developed for younger children who were at risk for foster care drift, concurrent planning replaces the sequential approach to case planning.[19] An alternative permanency goal is pursued at the same time as reunification. In some jurisdictions, foster parents are specially trained to serve as *resource parents*— able to support the biological parents' efforts towards reunification, but also able and willing to become adoptive parents if reunification efforts are unsuccessful.[20]

Concurrent case planning works well with young children.[21] Resource parents of very young children are often positioned to become role models for the biological parents, serving as parenting coaches and mentors. Because the lines of communication and interaction are much more open, parents can be more involved in the daily lives of their infants and can learn from more seasoned foster parents. When reunification is not possible, the foster parent or relative is prepared to care for the child long term and essential attachments to primary caregivers are not interrupted by a change in permanency goal. Additionally, the relationship between substitute caregiver and parent may diminish the need for litigation and increase voluntary relinquishments. Optimally, when reunification is not feasible, this less acrimonious process allows the infant to maintain relationships with the key people in his life, even after adoption.

How Concurrent Planning Benefits Very Young Children[1]

Very young children are the least likely to be reunified and the most likely to be adopted. They also remain in care longer than their older counterparts. Concurrent planning, encouraged by ASFA, can support timely permanent outcomes while reducing young children's time in care. For concurrent planning to succeed, foster/adoptive families (also called resource families), must understand and distinguish between their multiple roles. They must be willing to make a long-term commitment to the child and mentor the birth family toward reunification. Two successful approaches to concurrent planning are discussed below.

Increasing Timely Permanency

Colorado's concurrent planning model began in the early 1990s and involves caseworkers who are intensively trained on concurrent case planning. Legislation supports expedited permanency, and state procedures and financial supports encourage frontloading services to families. Some jurisdictions use these supports to implement family group conferencing, family team meetings, or to purchase substance abuse or mental health services. Some jurisdictions assign two caseworkers to each family—one for the child and one for the parents.

Outcomes are favorable:

▶ 82% of children served attain permanency in one year.

▶ An additional 18% of children achieve permanency in around 15 months.

▶ Of 522 children for whom placement data was available:

    ▶ 77% were permanently placed within their family system, with more than 41% returning to the parent from whom they were removed;

    ▶ 9% were placed with another parent; and

    ▶ 26% were placed permanently with relatives.[2]

Decreasing Length of Stay

San Mateo County, California's concurrent planning practices developed from a family preservation model that the county began in 1980. Recognizing the growing numbers of very young children who were not being reunified, the county began using the foster/adoptive parent model. This model emphasizes identifying permanency resources early, fully involving the birth family, and committing to strong reunification efforts, including assessing the family's prognosis for reunification.

Data show that San Mateo County attains permanency for its children faster than the state as a whole:

▶ 74% of children were reunited within 12 months, compared with 65% statewide during 2003-2004.

▶ Equally important, 47% of adopted children achieved permanency within 12 months compared with 27% across the state.

The success of this model is attributed to buy-in from the child welfare administration and staff, the courts, and the community. Program managers stress that involving court and agency staff when designing and implementing the process is key.[3]

Sources:

1. This discussion was drawn from Child Information Gateway. *Concurrent Planning: What the Evidence Shows*, Washington, DC: U.S. Department of Health and Human Services, April 2005. Available at www.childwelfare.gov/pubs/issue_briefs/concurrent_evidence/index.cfm.

2. For more information about the Colorado model, contact the Child Welfare Division of the State Department of Human Services, 303/866-3278.

3. For more information about the San Mateo County model, contact San Mateo County Human Services, Children & Family Services—East Palo Alto Office, 650/363-4185.

Services

Identify the family's service needs.

Families and young children in the child welfare system have different strengths, challenges, and support systems. Thus, services will vary and should be tailored to each family's circumstances. Most very young children and their families involved with the child welfare system need services beyond those for substance abuse, domestic violence, or other critical needs. Such services may include child development and trauma reduction services, and treatments or interventions for the child. Because infants develop within the context of their primary relationships, interventions related to bonding and attachment, such as Child-Parent Psychotherapy, may be necessary for both the infant and parent. Many services for very young children are discussed in other chapters of this book.

Assessment-driven services

As with case planning, service needs should be driven by early assessments and screenings. It should be clearly stated who is responsible for taking an infant to therapies, treatments, doctor appointments, etc. The primary substitute caregiver and/or the parent should be required to support the infant during treatments and procedures and provide the treating professional with up-to-date information about the child.

Parenting courses

Once a parent has begun engaging in services to address the issues that brought the child into care, she can benefit from a comprehensive evidence-based parenting course. Parenting programs come in many shapes and sizes. Ideally, a parent of a child under age five should be enrolled in an evidence-based parenting program that includes a parent-child interactive component. Structured preservice and postservice behavioral observations and paper/pencil pre/post standardized and validated measures (e.g., the Adult Adolescent Parenting Inventory—AAPI) are useful tools for determining strengths and weakness and measuring growth over time.[22] Learning how to be a nurturing and safe parent is a dynamic process. An evidence-based parenting program can significantly improve a parent's caregiving abilities. Parents must be aware of basic child development as well as their roles and responsibilities in their child's life.

Features to look for in a parenting program for parents of very young children include that it:

- addresses areas specific to parenting very young children;
- uses a variety of teaching methods to accommodate different adult learning styles;
- emphasizes hands-on experiences (e.g., roleplaying, structured interaction with their child);
- assesses whether a parent is internalizing the information and can put what she has learned into practice rather than simply reporting on parent attendance;
- uses parenting facilitators to identify and build upon strengths and identify where a parent's lack of skills or knowledge can potentially harm a very young child; and
- respects the family's cultural identity.

Parenting programs geared for parents of very young children will target the skills and concepts needed to nurture, care for, and cope with the rapidly changing physical and emotional state of children ages zero to five. If a parent has other children over age five, the professionals in the case should consult and determine whether it is best to refer a parent to a parenting program that addresses the needs of each age range or focuses on younger children. The best programs tailor the course to the individual needs of the parent and his/her children.

Services for parents should target challenges that brought the family into the system and support their ability to connect with and care for their very young child. Despite the constraints of ASFA's timeframes, it is essential that parents of young children are not overburdened with multiple services and case plan requirements simultaneously. Rather, stagger services and ensure high quality, effective interventions are in place. Meanwhile, encourage parents to focus on quality interactions and visits with their child, and their ability to develop a safe, stable home environment.

Visitation and Family Time

Ensure a comprehensive visitation plan is developed.

Children develop within the context of their relationship with their primary caregivers. Children who are placed in care when they are between birth and three years of age are unable to use words to express their distress over losing their parents and often experience emotional disturbances.[23] Consistent contact between the parent and child increases the possibility of reunification, promotes healthy parent-child attachment, and mediates the negative effects of removal.[24] Visitation, or supervised visitation if appropriate, should be permitted unless the court determines that such visitation would place the child's life, health, or safety at risk. Family visits should take place in the least restrictive, most natural setting that can ensure the safety and well-being of the child.[25]

Quality visitation plans between young children, their parents, siblings, and extended family members directly relate to ASFA's requirement of timely permanency and reasonable efforts requirements. Visitation helps develop and support a parent's ability to care for the child. Consistent and positive interactions between a child and his or her parents indicate that a family is moving towards reunification. Likewise, inconsistent and negative parent-child contact shows a need for further service planning and interventions, addressing barriers to visitation, or reevaluating the permanency goal for the child. A well-crafted and supported visitation plan is essential to achieving permanency.[26]

Contact between parents and young children must be:
- frequent (multiple times a week);
- long enough to allow a range of experiences for the parent and child;
- consistent;
- connected to daily activities;
- in the least restrictive, most home-like setting; and
- conducive to meaningful parent-child interaction.

Because a normal parent-child relationship develops during daily activities such as diaper changes, dressing, bathing, and trips to the grocery store, visitation should not be the only activity to encourage a normal parent-child relationship. Judges should encourage parents to participate in scheduling and attending their child's doctor or specialist appointments and to interact with child care

Visitation and Permanency Planning

Visitation—"the heart of permanency planning"—is a key strategy for reunifying families and achieving permanency. To preserve and strengthen parent-child attachment, promote permanency, and reduce the potentially damaging effects of separation, attorneys who represent very young children in foster care or their parents should make visitation that ensures the child's safety and well-being a focus of their advocacy. Because children in foster care often come from families where the parent-child attachment is unhealthy, visitation should be viewed as a *planned, therapeutic intervention* and the best possible opportunity to begin to heal what may be a damaged or troubled relationship. In addition, visits offer a real-life opportunity to view parental capacity and provide critical information to the court about the parent-child relationship. In this regard, visitation is a *diagnostic tool* to help determine as quickly as possible if reunification is the best permanency option for the child.

Because the term *visitation* does not adequately describe the quality and quantity of time that families need to spend together when children are removed from the home, child welfare experts have begun using other terms, such as *family time, family access,* and *family interaction*. Research shows that regular, frequent visitation increases the likelihood of successful reunification, reduces time in out-of-home care, promotes healthy attachment, and reduces the negative effects of separation for the child and the parent.

Source:
Excerpted without citations from Smariga, Margaret. *Visitation with Infants and Toddlers in Foster Care: What Judges and Attorneys Need to Know*. Washington, DC: ABA Center on Children and the Law & Zero to Three, 2007. Available at www.abanet.org/child/policy-brief2.pdf.

providers. This supports reunification and helps the parent develop working relationships with health and child care providers.

When there are concerns about healthy attachment between a very young child and his parent, therapeutic visitation or Child-Parent Psychotherapy (CPP) may be appropriate. CPP is a relationship-based psychotherapy facilitated by a trained infant mental health clinician. It uses a structured therapeutic process to support healthy attachment and reciprocity between a parent and her very young child.[27]

A parent's incarceration should not prevent parent-child contact. If contact is in the child's best interests and can be safely arranged, especially if the parent is not a threat and is a potential long-term caregiver, efforts should be made to promote visitation. Some correctional institutions have units that allow mothers and their infants to stay together or special areas for very young children and their parents to visit in person. At the very least, photographs should be exchanged. Telephone, video conferencing, or other creative uses of technology may be appropriate depending on the child's age or developmental level.[28]

Visitation plans must be clearly described in the case plan and all involved in the case need to understand one another's roles and responsibilities regarding visitation. Parents, caseworkers, relatives, foster parents, and other providers of family support should be expected to help develop the visiting arrangements and support the plan.

Review Hearings

Key decisions and questions for the judge:[29]

▸ Is there a need for continued placement of the child?

▸ Does the court-approved, long-term permanent plan for the child remain the best plan?

▸ Is the agency making reasonable efforts to rehabilitate the family and eliminate the need for placing the child?

▸ Do services set forth in the case plan and the responsibilities of the parties need to be clarified or modified due to new information or changed circumstances?

▸ Is the child in an appropriate placement that adequately meets all physical, emotional, and educational needs?

▸ Do the terms of visitation or family time need to be modified?

▸ Do terms of child support need to be set or adjusted?

▸ Are additional orders needed to move the case toward successful completion?

▸ What timeframe should be set to achieve reunification or another permanent plan for the child?

Assessing the Permanency Plan

Assess whether the issues that caused the child's removal are being addressed.

The review hearing evaluates whether the parent is sufficiently engaged in remedial and supportive services and if those services continue to be appropriate. Although much focus is on parents and their compliance with the case plan, it is important to assess whether the child-placing agency has offered appropriate services to remedy the problem that caused the child to enter care.

Obtain information from service and treatment providers who have assessed the parent's progress and who can give information about the quality of parent-child interactions. If structured parent-child observations are occurring through therapeutic visitation or CPP, request the professional's assessment of the parent's ability to read the infant's cues, respond to the verbal child's request, or to follow their child's lead during play time. For example, ask case managers or relatives who supervise visits and other contact whether the parent talks to her infant, sets limits for the active preschooler, and responds appropriately and safely to a toddler's temper tantrums. This information will help determine whether the parent has internalized the skills and knowledge from her parenting program, therapy, or anger management course.

Therapists and other service providers should be encouraged to attend the review hearings or to submit a report detailing the parent's progress. At review hearings, directly address the parents and ask them to share what they have learned through their courses and any insights they have gained through their therapeutic interventions about how their choices and behavior affect the well-being of their young child.

Order additional services or reassessments for the child.

At each review hearing, determine whether the child is receiving necessary services and interventions to mitigate the impact of the maltreatment and support healthy growth and development while in care. Specific recommendations regarding these services are covered in previous chapters. An infant who entered care at two months of age is a completely different child at the first review hearing. By this point in the infant's development, he may be sitting up, starting to eat solid foods, or even be crawling. Deficits in performing normal developmental tasks may become more pronounced than when the case plan was first created and the infant was first assessed. Thus, judges can use the review hearing to order another developmental screen—such as the Ages & Stages questionnaire[30]—to identify developmental delays.

Evaluate safety and risk factors if the child will return home.

If reunification is being considered at this stage, safety and risk factors surrounding the return must be evaluated. Some tools to help focus the inquiry when very young children are involved include:

- **Quality observations of parent-child interactions and reports** from substitute caregivers, caseworkers, and service providers about the parent's ability to respond to the infant's needs and cues are essential. If no structured process for observing parent-child interactions (discussed earlier) exists, consider ordering such an observation by a skilled infant mental health specialist.

- **Observations regarding the parent's knowledge, skills, and ability to put these into practice** from all who observe the parent and child together. Their insights are good indicators of whether the infant will be safe and cared for upon his return to his parent.

- **Information about availability and use of intensive home-based services to support reunification.** A prereunification family group conference (discussed above) can identify and assess the family and community supports a parent can use when feeling overwhelmed or in need of assistance.

- **A clear plan identifying family and community resources that will support reunification** if intensive home-based services are not available.

If risk factors are present at the review hearing, evaluate the family's engagement in services and the kind of support they have been offered.

Seek information about why a parent is not engaged in services:
- Is transportation or logistics an issue?
- Do the services conflict with the parent's employment or education?
- Are the services still appropriate or have the parent or child's needs changed?
- Is the substitute caregiver working with and mentoring the parent or is she impeding the reunification process? If so, what are the substitute caregiver's concerns and suggestions to remedy them?

Parents of young children are also in a constant state of transition—learning new skills and modifying old ones—and they may need different services and supports than those anticipated five or six months ago.

Determine if the substitute caregiver supports the parent toward reunification.

Assuming a concurrent case plan is in effect, the review hearing offers an opportunity to address whether the caregiver supports the parent toward reunification. Seek assurance that the substitute caregiver remains able and willing to be a permanent caregiver if reunification is not likely. Address any service and support needs of the substitute caregiver as well. As an infant grows and develops into an active toddler, a caregiver who enjoys caring for infants may not be able to

Infant Visiting Checklist for Family Court Judges

Visiting Plan

▶ What is the current visiting arrangement? (Where? How frequent? How long? Who is present? Level of supervision?)

▶ Is this visiting plan frequent enough to build attachment between the infant and parent?

▶ Does this visiting arrangement allow the parent to parent? This includes changing and feeding the infant; learning about the infant's cries, habits, and growth; and keeping the child safe in real-life situations.

▶ Was the purpose of visits clearly communicated to the parent (meet the infant's needs, stimulate the child's growth and development, communicate love for and enjoyment of the child to the child, ease the toddler's adjustment to separation)?

▶ What are the beginning and the end of the visits like (infant's response, parent's response, source of this information, possible reasons for assessment if any negative reports, changes over time, efforts to ease the transition)?

▶ If there are other children living separately from the infant, have sibling visits been set up?

Evolution

▶ How long has this visiting arrangement been in place? If more than three months, why hasn't the arrangement progressed? Answers should be child-related (e.g., safety or developmental concerns) or related to the parent's ability to meet the child's needs— not punitive (e.g., parent has not followed through with referrals or completed service plan, parent relapsed three months ago).

Permanency

▶ Is this visiting plan moving the court closer to achieving the permanency goal? Whenever possible, are the visits close to real-life situations that will allow the parent to address real-life parenting challenges?

Parental Participation in Child's Life

▶ Is the parent participating in the infant's medical appointments, early intervention services, and other activities?

▶ Has attention been paid to arranging visits on birthdays, holidays, anniversaries, and other special occasions that may be important to the child, parent, and family?

▶ Is mutual communication facilitated between the parent and the foster parent regarding the infant's habits, routines, behavior, preferences, and development/ growth?

Limiting, Suspending, or Terminating Visits

Unless there is imminent risk to the infant's safety or well-being or evidence of visit-based harm, before suspending or limiting visits, consider the following:

▶ What is the basis of this request?

▶ Has adequate time and explanation of attachment building been given to the parent? Has the parent been encouraged to persistently, actively, and patiently build attachment with the infant? Have efforts to slowly wean the foster parent out of the visits been tried?

▶ For parents with substance abuse issues: Has the caseworker or substance abuse counselor discussed the expectations, parameters, and purpose of visits with the parent? Have they discussed relapse prevention to address the difficult underlying issues visits may present?

▶ If due to the parent's inconsistent attendance at visits: What efforts have been made to identify the reasons for irregular attendance? Have there been efforts to engage and support the parent to build an attachment with and parent her/his infant?

▶ If parental ambivalence toward resuming full-time care of the infant is assessed (including cases where the parent has prior termination of parental rights), has a referral for counseling about options been made?

Source:
Adapted with permission from Dicker, Sheryl and Tanya Krupat. "Permanent Judicial Commission on Justice for Children Infant Visiting Checklist for Family Court Judges." Unpublished draft. New York State Permanent Judicial Commission on Justice for Children, 2006.

supervise or care for a bustling two year old. She may require assistance enrolling the toddler in a quality early care and education program or financial assistance to buy a bed when the crib is no longer safe (especially for those toddlers who like to climb out in the middle of the night).

Modifying Visitation

Assess the visitation plan and whether changes are needed.

Review hearings are a good time to assess the quality of visits and explore whether changes are needed. Suspending visits between a developing infant and the parent when the parent is not participating consistently in visitation may significantly impact the relationship. Unless the child is at risk of harm or the visits have already harmed the child, it is important to understand why a parent is inconsistent with visitation. If a parent is ambivalent towards visitation after efforts to engage, encourage the parent to discuss available options with a therapist and attorney.[31]

If safety issues are not a concern, unsupervised contact or a living arrangement that allows around-the-clock contact (i.e., teen mother living in foster care with her infant; a residential treatment program; or a grandparent who has custody of the child and is allowed to have the parent reside in her home) may be the best way to support the infant's attachment to her primary caregiver while ensuring her safety. However, because many children in the foster care system generally do not experience healthy attachment relationships, visitation is ideally understood as a 'planned, therapeutic intervention' and should be constructed as such.[32]

If parent-child contact must be supervised for the safety of the child, such visits should be in as natural an environment as possible with age-appropriate toys that encourage parent-child interaction.[33] The supervisor should model appropriate parenting when a parent is struggling to interact with the child or behaving inappropriately. Supervisors need to be sensitive to the emotional needs of the infant and the parent related to their separation. If a parent does not understand his infant's needs or does not respond to the infant's cues, CPP should be considered.

Visitation logistics should be reassessed often. Is the parent struggling with visiting three different children in three locations? Is the visitation time interfering with the toddler's nap time? Is the parent able to juggle older children who are seeking her attention and a new infant who needs her focus as well? Because visitation is key to promoting attachment and bonding, extra care and attention should be devoted to ensuring the arrangements are feasible and promote successful parent-child interactions.

Permanency Hearings

ASFA prioritizes permanency options for children as follows:
1. reunification
2. adoption
3. guardianship
4. placement with a fit and willing relative
5. another planned permanent living arrangement (APPLA)

At the 12-month permanency hearing, judges must make key decisions about a child's permanent custody and specific dates for finalizing those arrangements. Judges must also determine whether to extend a child's stay in care for a specific period while continuing to pursue reunification with the parent(s).

Making a permanency determination for very young children after 12 months in care can be difficult. If permanency planning begins at the start of the case, the answer should be clear. For example:

- A parent who has engaged in services, visited intensively with her infant, and participated actively in her infant's early intervention and early care and education services should have already regained physical custody of her child by this stage. If not, the parent should be ready to regain custody at the permanency planning hearing.
- Adoption is optimal when a parent has not engaged in services or visitation or remedied the circumstances that brought the child into care. Ideally, the infant or toddler's substitute caregiver supports reunification and is willing to adopt if reunification becomes implausible. Often in this circumstance, a parent voluntarily relinquishes her parental rights and the adoptive parent allows ongoing contact.

These are the easy scenarios, when things fall into place naturally because planning, services, and supports started early and were reassessed and updated regularly. What is the best decision-making process when it is not as clearcut as these scenarios?

Reunification

Determine if reunification is a viable permanency plan.

Reunification is the preferred permanency option if the parent can keep the child safe and well. There is little research about the decision-making process related to reunification and what contributes to a *successful* reunification, especially when very young children are involved.[34] We do know that infants have the highest rate of postreunification maltreatment, with one in five reentering foster care, usually within 90 days.[35] These findings underscore the need to be careful and clear about carrying out this permanency option.[36] Factors that impact decisions to reunify a parent with a very young child include:

- quality of relationship between the parent and child;
- quality and frequency of parent-child interactions;
- parental compliance with services and benefits attained;
- long- or short-term special medical or developmental needs of the young child;
- parent's demonstrated understanding of the infant's needs;
- parent's capacity to meet the infant's needs;
- family and community supports available to support a parent and child;
- if there are siblings, the parent's track record in assuring the siblings' school attendance, medical appointments, and any required treatment;
- parental mental health and addiction issues;

- length of time out of the parent's care; and
- point at which the infant was removed (e.g., at birth, six months).

Identify how reunification will affect the child in the short term.

Research shows that for infants, changing caregivers is traumatic.[37] Reunification, or any transition, can have harmful short-term effects on the child, especially for those children between the ages of six and 24 months old.[38] Infants often form secure attachments to substitute caregivers who have loved them and have attended to their daily needs. The person an infant trusts most to continue caring for him is naturally the person who has been changing his diapers, feeding him, bathing him, putting him to bed, and so forth. Because an infant cannot understand why things have changed, removal from his substitute caregiver—even to a parent with whom there is a healthy attachment and relationship—may cause distress similar to the initial removal. Removal from substitute care often changes the infant's daily routine—a common source of security for the child. The longer the infant has been in out-of-home care and the more intense the attachment and sense of security associated with that placement, the more psychologically difficult the reunification process.[39] Supportive therapeutic services and transition planning must be considered to promote a successful reunification.

Ensure transition planning is part of a reunification plan.

To avoid another traumatic life event for the infant, *transition planning* should be part of any plan for reunification. Ideally, when reunification is the goal, parents and substitute caregivers will have developed a working relationship, allowing the young child to attach with both caregivers and to observe her primary caregivers connecting with each other.[40]

Any effort to increase the parent's daily caregiving and to nurture the relationship between the child and parent will support a smooth transition. The parent should begin taking on more tasks of daily care through increased visitation or involvement in the substitute caregiver's home. If comfortable, the substitute caregiver could visit the parent's home with the infant on the first few in-home visits, if those have not yet started. Maintaining the status quo in other aspects of the infant's life during the transition phase—child care, therapists, babysitters, doctors—can ease the process and minimize any distress. Finally, ensuring that the parent is aware of the infant's schedule and routine and has a plan to reinforce some of this structure may help the infant better cope with the changes.

Adoption

Determine if adoption is a viable permanency plan.

When a child will not reunify with a parent, adoption is the next best permanency option. In fact, infants represent 48% of adopted children.[41] For an infant who is attached to a foster parent or relative, adoption can formalize this primary relationship in the infant's life. Data on outcomes for infants adopted from the child welfare system are scarce.[42] That said, infants who have been adopted from the child welfare system exhibit better outcomes than their counterparts who remain in care, although this may be due to the instability of foster care rather than the adoptive family.[43]

For infants not already placed with caregivers who are able and willing to adopt (or take some other form of long-term legal guardianship), legally freeing the infant for adoption through a termination of parental rights (TPR) proceeding often extends the time he will spend in care. Once the TPR is finalized, children without an identified adoptive parent may remain in legal limbo while one is identified. One study found that "a surprising number of infants who are placed in child welfare care are neither reunified with their families nor readily placed in alternative permanent homes."[44]

These findings speak to the need to concurrently plan for reunification and possible long-term permanent placement with a specific substitute caregiver from the start of the case. After a TPR, the court should hold frequent review hearings—every two to three months—to determine whether sufficient efforts are being made to identify and secure an adoptive home for a legally free young child.

Determine if the current caregiver can adopt the child.

If adoption is the desired permanency option, confirm that the current caregiver:

- is willing to adopt, and
- would be approved as an adoptive parent.

If concurrent planning was implemented on day one, and if an adoption quality home study was conducted at the start of the case, these critical questions will already be answered. Furthermore, if an extensive search and review of relatives took place early in the case, as some state laws and now federal law require,[45] the child's 'preadoptive' placement should not be disrupted by relatives who step forward after the TPR stage. Remember, there is great psychological risk to disrupting a child's secure attachments without compelling evidence that doing so is clearly in the child's best interest.

If the current caregiver no longer wishes to adopt, determine whether she would be willing to be a permanent guardian through a legal guardianship proceeding (see below). Also assess the caregiver's ability and desire to adequately care for the infant as he grows. If the current caregiver is unwilling or unable to care for the child permanently, require the state to provide a full analysis of other immediate permanency options through adoption or guardianship with family members or nonrelatives.

Consider ordering mediation to resolve adoption-related concerns.

Once a TPR petition is filed, it may be beneficial to order the parties to attend mediation. Mediation can clarify issues in the case, help parents decide whether voluntarily relinquishing their parental rights is in their best interest, and explore whether open adoption will take place. If an infant is with a relative or foster parent who is willing to permit informal or formal (through an open adoption) post-adoption contact between the biological parent and/or family, a voluntary relinquishment will speed the TPR process and allow for adoption.

Legal Guardianship

Determine if legal guardianship is a viable permanency plan.

Legal guardianship is defined by the ASFA regulations as "a judicially created relationship between child and caretaker which is intended to be permanent and self-sustaining as evidenced by the transfer to the caretaker" of certain parental rights, "with respect to the child" including "protection, education, care and control of the person and decision making."[46] A relative or nonrelative can become a legal guardian and, according to ASFA, that legal guardianship must be binding beyond the jurisdiction of the court hearing the dependency case. In some states, legal guardianship dissolves the dependency court's jurisdiction altogether.[47]

Legal guardianship is a good alternative to adoption when there are no grounds for TPR and a caregiver is willing to serve in this capacity permanently. Establishing a permanent legal guardianship for a very young child rather than a nonpermanent arrangement with a relative benefits an infant or toddler in the long run. Many relative caregivers prefer this option over adoption because they do not want the parent's rights to be severed or to be a part of an adversarial termination of parental rights process. Judges can ask about the relative's ability—physically and emotionally—to care for a very young child through the age of majority.

Federal law now permits states to enter into kinship guardianship assistance agreements with relatives who are serving as foster parents to their kin using Title IV-E funds.[48] This means that relative caregivers in this circumstance could continue to receive foster care maintenance payments, even after a permanent guardianship is established.

Permanent guardianship may be a good alternative for a developmentally delayed or very young parent. This option supports permanency, but allows a parent who is incapable of change for reasons beyond their control (e.g., cognitive delay) to retain her rights and to actively contribute to her child's upbringing. Additionally, children of parents with disabilities may be entitled to certain benefits, and terminating the legal relationship would end the child's right to receive such benefits (e.g., social security disability payments).

Placement with a Fit and Willing Relative

Determine if relative placement is a viable permanency plan, only after exploring more desirable options.

If neither reunification, adoption, nor legal guardianship is in the best interests of the child, next consider a placement with a fit and willing relative. Although the relative must commit to caring for the child until the age of majority, this option is akin to legal limbo for very young children. In fact, the preamble to ASFA states that "relative placements should not preclude consideration of legalizing the permanency of the placement through adoption or legal guardianship."[49] State statutes typically do not allow this permanency option unless certain conditions are met. States must continue to supervise the placement and the court must review the case regularly (i.e., every six months) and conduct permanency hearings to reevaluate the possibility of adoption or legal guardianship.

For very young children, placement with a fit and willing relative should only be accepted when a more legally permanent arrangement is not in the child's best interest. Judges should require regular updates on efforts to identify an adoptive parent or to help the relative seek a legal guardianship. Additionally, because this option does not preclude a parent from regaining custody, judges should closely consider the same questions that would be asked when assessing reunification.

Another Planned Permanent Living Arrangement (APPLA)

In most cases, APPLA should not be a permanency goal for very young children.

ASFA was developed to prevent children from living their lives in foster or group homes. The preamble advises that long-term placement in a licensed foster home should be the very last resort, and the regulations require the state to document a 'compelling reason' for choosing APPLA as a permanency option.[50] These compelling reasons as applied to very young children may include:

- when a parent and child share a significant bond, but the parent is unable to care for the child due to an emotional or physical disability, or
- when an Indian tribe has identified another planned permanent living arrangement for the child.[51]

APPLA is not a suitable permanency outcome for a very young child. Even when the parent is disabled and unable to care for a child to whom there is a significant bond, the judge should ensure the foster parents are informed of the benefits of becoming the child's adoptive parent and/or legal guardian. Parent-child relationships may be maintained through open adoptions or visitation agreements in a guardianship order. If a foster parent has concerns about covering the costs of a medically fragile or special needs infant and requires the foster care payment to offset certain costs, request that a state and federal benefits and entitlements expert meet with the foster parents and caseworker to secure financial support so a more permanent legal arrangement is possible.

Note that under the Indian Child Welfare Act (ICWA), the permanency preferences of ASFA are not the same. Relatives and *extended families* are preferred over adoption, and many tribes do not value adoption in the same way as ASFA does. Additionally, APPLA can be more easily used as a permanency option for children who are covered by ICWA.[52]

Consulting the Child

Hear the child's views regarding the permanency plan.

The Social Security Act, which includes Title IV-E funding to the states for children in foster care, requires that the court holding a permanency hearing conduct an age-appropriate consultation with the child.[53] This requirement is met when the court obtains the *views of the child in the context of the permanency hearing*.[54] In other words, while it may not be possible for a court to hear testimony from a very young, preverbal child, the court should hear about the child's views on his or her permanency plan and incorporate this information into the overall decision-making process.

A report written by a nonattorney or CASA, a caseworker's testimony, and communications by the legal representative for the child may present the child's view; however, information relating to the child's best interests alone is not enough to satisfy this 'consultation' requirement.[55] Some states provide guidance to attorneys and other child welfare professionals about determining a child's view on his or her permanency plan. Generally, *age appropriate* means "meeting the cognitive level of a child for their developmental age" unless a child is cognitively delayed.[56]

Observe preverbal children in court to inform your decision making.

Even when a very young child is preverbal, there are many benefits to bringing an infant or toddler to hearings on a regular basis. The information gained from simply observing a child at a court hearing is invaluable. You can gain tremendous insight from seeing the young child interact with her parent and caregivers, and it gives the parent and child an opportunity to visit if the child is placed out of the home. Having a child present in the courtroom can also highlight how quickly she is growing and just how important speedy, decisive action towards permanency is. Courtroom observations can also help inform decisions about placement, visitation, or therapeutic services.

Consider the child's developmental stage during courtroom observations.

It is important to be familiar with developmental milestones when observing very young children. For infants and young children from birth to 12 months old, permanency observations might include:[57]

- How does the child interact and respond to caregivers, parents, and guardians?
- Is the child meeting developmental milestones?
- Does the child appear healthy and well-cared for?

Observations of toddlers and preschoolers in the courtroom might also include:[58]

- How does the child act when answering questions (if verbal)?
- Who does the child look to for help answering questions?
- Is he scared? Anxious? Avoidant?
- Does he look to the caregiver for the "right" answer?

A verbal child's presence in the courtroom also provides an opportunity to ask her questions. Use simple language, speak slowly, and allow the child time to process the question. Younger children can better understand concrete terms and will recognize names better than pronouns. Possible questions to ask might include:

- How old are you?
- Do you like where you are staying now?
- Do you go to preschool or daycare? What things do you like to do at school?
- Do you feel sad or miss anyone? (e.g., brother, sisters, grandparents)
- Have you been to the doctor?
- Do you like the doctor?[59]

Extending the Goal of Reunification

Determine if there is cause to extend the goal of reunification.

It may be that by the time of the permanency hearing a parent is progressing towards reunification, but barriers to taking physical custody of the child are still present (e.g., housing). The federal regulations state that if a child has been placed in out-of-home care for 15 of the preceding 22 months, the state must file to TPR unless there is a compelling reason not to file. While ASFA's reduced timeframes and required permanency hearings stress that time is of the essence for children, overcoming addiction and becoming stable, even when diligently pursued, takes time—often more than 12 months.

When there is cause to extend the timeframe for reunification, evaluate the probability of reunification by assessing a parent's progress with their key services and the consistency and quality of the parent-child interactions. When extending the goal of reunification past the permanency hearing is necessary, the time given to a parent to complete case plan tasks and establish that they have remedied the circumstances that brought the child into care should be consistent with the child's developmental needs.[60] Thus, for an infant placed in foster care, the extension would be short—a matter of weeks. For a preschooler in the care of his grandmother, it may be appropriate to allow the parent several months to finalize reunification-related tasks.

Unless a parent was simply not offered services, refrain from continuing the goal of reunification when a parent has only become engaged in services and visitation in the months or weeks leading up to the permanency hearing. Rather, look for a "genuine, sustainable investment in completing the requirements of the case plan in order to retain reunification as the permanency goal."[61]

Postpermanency Support for Young Children and Their Families

The ability of permanent caregivers to maintain a safe and nurturing environment is critical to achieving sustainable outcomes for very young children exiting the child welfare system. Certain circumstances make infants highly vulnerable to reentry into care for even longer periods. Infants who are reunified in a fairly short period (three months) are more likely to reenter care than older children and other infants who remain in care longer.[62] In addition, infants who return to care a second time stay longer in care than their first experience.[63] Appropriate postpermanency supports can help avoid such reentries. Supports for permanent caregivers should be developed, ideally through a family group conferencing or decision-making process, early in the case and updated regularly as circumstances for the child and her family change.

Sustaining Reunification

Ensure supports are in place to sustain reunification.

Before reunification and during the postplacement supervision period, require case managers and family members to:
- Identify barriers to successful reunification.
- Identify supports to address and overcome reunification barriers.
- Develop a safety or emergency plan to help the parent cope with parenting stressors and challenges that could compromise successful reunification.

Other reunification supports that should be in place before discharge/termination of supervision:
- Connect the birth family with a medical and dental home (as discussed in Chapter 2) and promote the family's *health literacy* (their ability to understand health information).
- Ensure the parents and other family members are aware of the child's special needs and special treatments or appointments. Connections should be made between the parent and the provider well before case closure.
- Develop a visitation plan if only one parent is given custody but the other is permitted to maintain contact with the child.
- Enroll the family in financial assistance programs (e.g., Medicaid, food stamps, Temporary Aid to Needy Families (TANF)).
- Ensure all entitlements and subsidies are in place before case closure.

- Confirm that the parent has identified people or agencies to turn to for respite care, babysitting, and general parenting questions. These should be written down and include specific names and contact numbers.
- Confirm that a parent is linked to neighborhood supports through a community or neighborhood center (e.g., YMCA); link with possible afterschool/summer supports.
- Ensure the parent is engaged in peer support groups for chronic issues such as substance abuse or domestic violence. Some parenting programs offer 'booster sessions' and support groups once a parent completes the program.
- Ensure the child is enrolled in child care or Early Head Start/Head Start and the enrollment package is completed before exiting care. A meeting between the director and child care center caregivers should be facilitated if contact has not already been made.
- Confirm the parent has secured stable housing and employment or a source of income (e.g., child support, Supplemental Security Income) before the case is closed. Make sure he has a backup plan if housing or employment plans do not work out.
- Ensure the parent is connected with the early intervention provider well before reunification and case closure.
- Devise a placement plan if there is a relapse, another incident, or the parent is incarcerated.
- Determine a safety plan for the adult victim and for the child in domestic violence cases.

Sustaining Adoption

Identify adoption disruption factors.

Adoptions are generally highly successful permanency arrangements, although some adopted children and their families confront difficulties.[64] Even so, adopting a very young child from the foster care system can be challenging due to the impact on the child's development by the initial maltreatment, trauma, and resulting stay in foster care.

Research shows several factors increase the risk of adoption disruption:

- **Child's age**—The older the child is when adopted, the higher the likelihood for disruption—an encouraging finding for families who adopt very young children.[65]

- **Alcohol/drug exposure**—Adoptions of children with prenatal alcohol exposure are at risk for placement disruptions because these children are more likely to experience multiple psychiatric symptoms as they mature. However, low placement disruptions have been found in drug-exposed children adopted early in life (before eight years old).[66]

- **Inexperienced/unknown adoptive caregivers**—Adoptions by strangers or families without adoption or foster care experience are at higher risk of disrupting.[67] Thus it is important for child-placing agencies to be upfront with prospective adoptive parents about a child's special needs and the treatment for those needs. Adoption by someone unknown to a very young child can be frightening. Adoptive parents of very young children should not be lulled into a false sense of security by believing the infant will "just adjust" because she does not understand what is going on. Those adopting very young children must understand early child development and the potential for a very difficult transition phase with a lot of crying, anxiety, rejection, and sleepless nights.

Identify postadoption supports.

Although there is minimal research on postadoption support services, evidence suggests that a family-focused, long-term intervention is a more effective form of postadoption support than short-term interventions.[68] Self-help and adoptive parent support groups fit the needs of many adoptive parents.

Judges should ensure the child-placing agency provides the following postadoption services to families:[69]

Educational/informational:

- full disclosure of information about the infant, including medical, developmental/mental health, social, and genetic history;
- literature related to the infant's specific needs and about adopting very young children;
- lectures, trainings, workshops to help build skills around parenting an infant and about adoption issues;
- support groups and adoptive parent mentors to help them address their child's specific needs;
- Life Book (if available)—a record of an adoptive child's life told through photos, artwork, mementos, and stories that is developed starting when the child enters care.

Clinical:

- couple or family counseling to help cope with the impact of adoption;
- reliable, high quality respite care.

Material:

- adoption subsidies should be applied before the final adoption order (one study found that adoptive families who received higher subsidies were more likely to be maintained than those who received lower subsidies and that families that did not receive any subsidy were more likely to experience a disrupted adoption);[70]
- medical care and a medical home;
- educational opportunities (e.g., Head Start/Early Head Start; child care subsidies).

Permanent Placement with a Relative or Nonrelative

Ensure postadoption supports and services are equally available to permanent guardians or long-term relative caregivers.

Many of the child-focused supports for reunification and adoption apply to sustaining any permanent placement.

Maintain family connections.

The child benefits from maintaining as many connections as possible—to child care, primary care doctors and dentists, infant mental health and early intervention therapists. Nonrelative permanent caregivers should consider the infant's connection with her family of origin and her cultural heritage. A nonrelative should be willing to commit to sibling visits and family contact when feasible and in the infant's best interest. Even very young children benefit from exposure to their cultures of origin. When they grow up and have questions and concerns about where they come from, early exposure to food, music and customs will provide a framework. Contact with the birth family can also support this and maintain important sibling ties.

Conclusion

With ASFA providing the legal framework and the *RESOURCE GUIDELINES* advising on key questions and decisions during each step of the process, you have promising tools to promote timely, stable permanency for very young children in the child welfare system. By understanding early child development principles and research about how very young children experience removal, placement, reunification, and adoption, you can ensure the child welfare system holistically meets their physical, cognitive, and social-emotional needs.

Young children in care should always be viewed through an early child development lens. When possible and safe, keep children with their parent with intensive supports, education, and interventions. If removal is essential, require that every effort is made to ensure the young child's first placement will be the only placement if reunification becomes untenable. Using concurrent case planning is one element of that process. Require thoughtful, comprehensive visitation plans and hold all parties—parents, caregivers and state agencies—accountable for following such plans.

Whether your jurisdiction has a formal family group conferencing structure or not, expect parents, family members, and service providers to participate in case planning, fully support the goals, and increase the potential for successful reunification. Emphasize to parents, family members, and caseworkers that they are all responsible for the very young child's experience in the child welfare system, whether she achieves permanency in a timely manner, and whether her involvement in the system enhances her overall well-being.

Endnotes

1. Wulczyn, F., K.B. Hislop and B.J. Harden. "The Placement of Infants in Foster Care." *Infant Mental Health Journal* 23(5), 2002, 454-475, 456.

2. Jones Harden, B. *Infants in the Child Welfare System: A Developmental Framework for Policy and Practice*. Washington, DC: Zero to Three, 2007, 107.

3. P.L. 108-36

4. Jones Harden, 2007, 17.

5. Ibid.

6. *RESOURCE GUIDELINES: Improving Court Practice in Child Abuse & Neglect Cases*. Reno, NV: National Council of Juvenile and Family Court Judges, 1995. The *RESOURCE GUIDELINES* have been endorsed by the American Bar Association and the National Conference of Chief Justices.

7. For further guidance, the *ADOPTION AND PERMANENCY GUIDELINES: Improving Court Practice in Child Abuse and Neglect Cases*, published by the National Council of Juvenile and Family Court Judges, 2000, is an excellent resource that delves more deeply into considerations for timely permanency and adoption.

8. Ibid., 37. Some questions include changes to reflect a more specific focus on very young children.

9. Lillas, C., Judge L. Langer and M. Drinane. "Addressing Infant and Toddler Issues in the Juvenile Court: Challenges for the 21st Century." *Juvenile and Family Court Journal*, Spring 2004, 92.

10. For example, Promise Home in Tucson, AZ (http://thegivingtreeoutreach.org/id15.html) and the FACT (Fathers and Children Together) Program in Minneapolis, MN provide transitional housing for men and their children, and The Village South in Miami, FL provides residential substance abuse treatment to fathers or mothers with their children (www.villagesouth.com/fit.html).

11. Smariga, Margaret. *Visitation with Infants and Toddlers in Foster Care: What Judges and Attorneys Need to Know*. Washington, DC: ABA Center on Children and the Law & Zero to Three, 2007. Available at www.abanet.org/child/policy-brief2.pdf.

12. *RESOURCE GUIDELINES*, 1995, 57-58. Some questions include changes to reflect a more specific focus on very young children.

13. Jones Harden, 2007, 86.

14. Jurisdictions in California, Florida and Washington have instituted family finding as a standalone program or have implemented some of the tools. Visit www.senecacenter.org for more information about family finding and to request training for your jurisdiction.

15. Buie, J. and G.P. Mallon. "Achieving Permanency for Children & Youth Through Skillful Case Planning: Some Lessons Learned from Child & Family Service Review Final Reports." *Permanency Planning Today*, Summer 2002, 2-3.

16. This is also referred to as family team decision making or family group decision making.

17. Robinson, Judge S.D. et al. "Family Conferencing: A Success for Our Children." *Juvenile and Family Court Journal*, Fall 2002, 43-47, 45-46.

18. Ibid., 43-44.

19. U.S. Department of Health and Human Services, Administration for Children and Families, Administration on Children, Youth and Families, Children's Bureau. "Concurrent Planning: What the Evidence Shows." *Child Welfare Information Gateway Issue Brief*, April 2005. Available at www.childwelfare.gov/pubs/issue_briefs/concurrent_evidence/index.cfm.

20. Ibid.

21. Ibid.

22. This model has been developed in Miami-Dade County, FL as a collaboration between the child welfare community advisory committee, the dependency court (Judge Cindy Lederman), the child welfare system leadership and community parenting program providers in partnership with Dr. Lynne Katz (University of Miami) and Dr. Joy Osofsky (Louisiana State University). For more information about the AAPI, visit www.nurturingparenting.org.

23. Smariga, M., 2007, 5.

24. Ibid., 6.

25. Ibid., 11.

26. Ibid., 8.

27. Child-Parent Psychotherapy is discussed more fully in Chapter 3.

28. "Connecting Children with Incarcerated Parents." *Child Protection Best Practices Bulletin: Innovative Strategies to Achieve Safety, Permanence and Well-Being*. Available at www.f2f.ca.gov/res/pdf/ChildProtectionBPBulletins.pdf.

29. *RESOURCE GUIDELINES*, 1995, 70.

30. The Ages and Stages Questionnaire is a standardized parent report tool used for developmental surveillance for children 4–60 months of age. The parent-completed instruments address children's skills in four domains: language, personal-social, motor, and cognition. D. Bricker and J. Squires. "Ages and Stages Questionnaire." Available at www.brookespublishing.com/tools/asq. For other common developmental screening tools, see www.dbpeds.org/articles/detail.cfm?textid=539.

31. Smariga, 2007, 21.

32. Ibid., 7.

33. Ibid., 13.

34. Jones Harden, 2007, 104.

35. Ibid., 107.

36. U.S. Department of Health and Human Services, Administration on Children, Youth and Families. *Child Maltreatment 2006* (Washington, DC: U.S. Government Printing Office, 2008).

37. Jones Harden, 2007, 242.

38. Ibid.

39. Gauthier, Y., G. Fortin and G. Jéliu. "Clinical Application of Attachment Theory in Permanency Planning for Children in Foster Care: The Importance of Continuity of Care." *Infant Mental Health Journal* 25(4), 2004, 379-396, 386.

40. Jones Harden, 2007, 244.

41. Administration for Children and Families, 2006b.

42. Jones Harden, 2007, 108.

43. Ibid., 110.

44. Kemp, S.P. and J.M. Bodonyi. "Infants Who Stay in Foster Care: Child Characteristics and Permanency Outcomes of Legally Free Children First Placed as Infants." *Child and Family Social Work* 5, 2000, 102.

45. Fostering Connections to Success and Increasing Adoptions Act of 2008, P.L. 110-351.

46. 45 C.F.R. § 1355.20(a).

47. Ratterman Baker, D. et al. *Making Sense of the ASFA Regulations: A Roadmap for Effective Implementation.* Edited by D.B. Rauber. Washington, DC: ABA Center on Children and the Law, 2001, 94.

48. Fostering Connections to Success and Increasing Adoptions Act of 2008, P.L. 110-351.

49. 65 C.F.R. § 4060.

50. 45 C.F.R. §§ 1355.20(a) and 1356.21(h)(3).

51. 45 C.F.R. § 356.21(h)(3)

52. Ratterman Baker et al, 2001, 103; Jones, B.J., M. Tilden and K. Gaines-Stoner. *The Indian Child Welfare Act Handbook: A Legal Guide to the Custody and Adoption of Native American Children*, 2d ed. Chicago, IL: American Bar Association, 2008.

53. Social Security Act, § 475(5)(C)(ii).

54. U.S. Department of Health and Human Services, Administration for Children and Families, Administration on Children, Youth and Families, Children's Bureau. *Child Welfare Policy Manual.* Washington, DC, March 21, 2008. Available at www.acf.hhs.gov/j2ee/programs/cb/laws/cwpm/policy_dsp_pf.jsp?citID=58.

55. Ibid.

56. National Resource Center on Family Centered Practice and Permanency Planning. "Age-Appropriate Consultation" (power point presentation). September 2007. Available at www.dphhs.mt.gov/cfsd/.

57. "Engaging Young Children in the Courtroom: Judicial Bench Card." Washington, DC: ABA Center on Children and the Law, 2008. Available at www.abanet.org/child/empowerment/youthincourt.shtml.

58. "Engaging Toddlers and Preschoolers in the Courtroom: Judicial Bench Card." Washington, DC: ABA Center on Children and the Law, 2008. Available at www.abanet.org/child/empowerment/youthincourt.shtml.

59. Ibid.

60. U.S. Department of Health and Human Services, March 2008.

61. Ibid.

62. Wulczyn, F. "Caseload Dynamics and Foster Care Reentry." *Social Service Review*, 65, 1991, 133-156.

63. Kemp and Bodonyi, 2000.

64. Barth, R.P. and J.M. Miller. "Building Effective Post-Adoption Services: What is the Empirical Foundation?" *Family Relations* 49(4), 2000, 447-455, 447.

65. Ibid., 449.

66. Ibid.

67. Ibid.

68. Ibid., 450.

69. Ibid., 452.

70. Ibid.

chapter 5

A Call to Action: Improving the Court's Response

A Call to Action: Improving the Court's Response

How to the Improve Handling of Cases Involving Very Young Children

▶ Serve as a community leader.

▶ Convene a court-based group to focus on child welfare cases involving very young children.

▶ Testify or publicly advocate for policies or legislation.

▶ Educate the public.

▶ Participate on committees and other professional groups.

How to Lead Successful Court-Community Collaborations

▶ Exercise your leadership.

▶ Seek research-based reforms.

▶ Seek procedural enhancements.

▶ Ensure services are child-focused.

▶ Evaluate, evaluate, evaluate.

The lives of very young children are profoundly affected by the decisions you make every day in your courtroom. This guide shares knowledge about early brain development, healthy attachment, and other health and developmental considerations in cases involving very young children. With this knowledge, you have many opportunities to influence not only the individual cases you see every day, but also systemic changes that will improve outcomes for the youngest children in the child welfare system.

How to the Improve Handling of Cases Involving Very Young Children

Your decision-making role as a juvenile and family court judge is critical to the safety and well-being of very young children, their families, and their communities. You know well your responsibility to ask the right questions, require the right assessments and services, and demand accountability from service providers, child welfare agencies, and the lawyers appearing in your courtroom. What can you do in your role off the bench to advocate for system improvements that will improve outcomes for court-involved families?

The National Council of Juvenile and Family Court Judges has long called on its member judges to serve in a broader role that includes leadership in assessing the needs of children in the court and acting as advocates and catalysts for change in developing resources and implementing policies and procedures:

> Family court judges must take a leadership role to improve the administration of justice for children and families within the courts, in their communities, state capitols, and nationally. It is essential for family court judges to be active in the development of policies, laws, rules and standards by which these courts and their allied agencies and systems function.[1]

Not only can you be a powerful voice within the court system, you are also uniquely positioned to know the problems faced by the children and families who come before you every day. As a prominent and influential member of the community, you can help identify the unmet needs of very young children and their families, which in turn will benefit your community.

You can engage in a variety of activities that promote the administration of justice within your state's judicial code of conduct. These activities benefit the court, the community, and the children and families the court serves:[2]

Serve as a community leader.

Your leadership can help identify unmet needs of very young children in the court system and the services needed to address those needs. For instance, there is growing awareness of the need for early, preventative dental care for very young children in foster care. In your leadership role, you can help raise attention to this issue and reach out to community health centers or local dental care providers to identify services for infants and toddlers in care.

Convene a court-based group to focus on child welfare cases involving very young children.

Many judges have acted as community leaders to establish a variety of court-related services and programs, including court appointed special advocate (CASA) programs, family drug treatment courts, and specialized courts focusing on the unique needs of infants and toddlers in the court system.[3]

Testify or publicly advocate for policies or legislation.

Juvenile court judges have testified before state legislatures on issues such as the value of subsidized adoptions, the benefit of statewide child representation models, and the need for appropriate and sufficient reunification services. You can share your views based on your judicial experience by consulting with or testifying before local, state or national legislative or executive branch officials. You can also encourage support for adequate resources to provide the services needed by very young children in the court system. Many judicial professional organizations provide an avenue for this type of testimony or consultation.

Educate the public.

Share issues related to very young children by speaking before community and civic groups, writing newsletter articles or letters to the editor, and writing articles for scholarly journals that can influence the work of other courts. Educating the public about the need for parent-child psychotherapy or other services that promote positive parenting can bolster support for such programs within the community. If you have established a special court-based program or service for very young children in your court (such as a family drug court for parents of infants and toddlers), describing such efforts through professional journals can help other judges replicate successful programs in their own courts.

Participate on committees and other professionals groups.

You can join professional groups and committees that address the needs of court-involved children. Groups exist at the national level (such as the National Council of Juvenile and Family Court Judges or the American Bar Association's Judicial Division) and the state level. State judicial associations can have a significant impact on legislation and policy impacting the needs of children. Your state supreme court may have a commission or committee on foster care or other related issues where your expertise could help shape the state's response to very young children in care.

How to Lead Successful Court-Community Collaborations

Several courts around the country have implemented special dockets or courtroom procedures in response to the unique needs of infants, toddlers, and preschoolers. Successful approaches apply research to court practice to improve outcomes for very young, maltreated children. If your court has or is considering such a collaboration, your leadership and participation are key.

Healing the Youngest Children: Model Court-Community Partnerships,[4] which describes the court-community collaborations in depth, identifies 13 components that help fuel their success. These components address systems change, a focus on services for very young children, procedural enhancements, and sustainability efforts. You play a vital role in each. Here's how:

Exercise your leadership.

The systems change component depends on a strong, proactive judge who leads the court's efforts focusing on very young children. Therefore, you play an essential role marshaling community services and assistance for young children and their families. You also have a unique ability to encourage action among public and private child-serving agencies. For example, convening a meeting to address the availability of parent and child mental health services in your community could bring together not only advocates for each of the parties in child welfare cases but also mental health service providers throughout the community.

Your strong judicial leadership draws on the assets of all the collaborative partners to support the mutual goals and efforts of the program. In addition to the court, it is essential to work with the child welfare agency, early childhood specialists, and attorneys who know how the special needs of very young children should guide their requests for services on behalf of their clients.

Seek research-based reforms.

Any coordinated effort or intervention to improve outcomes for very young children in the child welfare system should be based on sound research. Enlisting early childhood experts and other knowledgeable parties is therefore essential. Equally important is developing tools to help identify gaps in local services and monitor how any intervention is affecting children's well-being and progress. For instance, child-parent psychotherapy shows promising early outcomes for safe reunification of young children with their parents. The collaborating entities should assess whether the community has the capacity to provide sufficient mental health interventions for the parent and child together, and if not, pursue ways in which such therapy could be offered. Judges can inform the community about gaps in services and mobilize community leaders and resources to address those gaps.

Seek procedural enhancements.

Core components that fall under procedural enhancements include many that you influence directly. For instance, the frequency of case review hearings can be set from the bench. Time between review hearings should be shortened and used productively. Frequent case reviews ensure that very young children receive services that are effective and age-appropriate. Regular meetings of the collaborative team members can also help ensure case progress.

Ensure services are child-focused.

As a judge, you can also ensure the services you order are child-focused. Implement concurrent planning requirements; ensure the case plan provides frequent, regular visits; ensure all necessary services are ordered for every young child; and order evidenced-based services to meet the family's needs. You can also use your position within the court to support ongoing training and assistance for legal and child-serving professionals working in your courtrooms to learn about the impact of abuse and neglect on early development.

Evaluate, evaluate, evaluate.

Finally, you can request ongoing evaluation of efforts to improve outcomes for infants, toddlers, and preschoolers. Routine evaluation is essential to identify whether court deadlines are being met, appropriate services are being offered and provided, or if gaps in services exist. Evaluation can also help support additional funding requests.

Now is the Time to Act

By implementing the recommended practice tips provided in this guide, you can ensure they become common practice among the nation's juvenile dependency courts. Always demand complete and current information about the health status of the infants, toddlers, and preschoolers who come before you and ensure that their needs are met. Continue to identify innovative approaches to address the health and developmental needs of very young children involved in the child welfare and court systems.

Please share this guide with other judges and advocates in your community. Judges, judicial officers, court administrators, attorneys, guardians ad litem, social workers, medical and health professionals, and others working with very young children can work together to create court systems that serve the specific needs of infants, toddlers, and preschoolers. Working together, you can improve both their immediate well-being and their long-term health and permanency outcomes.

Endnotes

1. National Council of Juvenile and Family Court Judges. *Children and Families First: A Mandate for America's Courts*, 1993, 4.

2. *A Judge's Guide to Improving the Legal Representation of Children.* Edited by K. Grasso. Washington, DC: ABA Center on Children and the Law, 1998, 13.

3. Hudson, L. et al. *Healing the Youngest Children: Model Court-Community Partnerships.* Washington, DC: ABA Center on Children and the Law and Zero to Three, 2007.

4. Ibid.

Author Biographies

American Bar Association
Center on Children and the Law

The ABA Center on Children and the Law, a program of the Young Lawyers Division, aims to improve children's lives through advances in law, justice, knowledge, practice and public policy. The Center's HRSA-funded Improving Understanding of Maternal and Child Health Project seeks to enable legal professionals to improve health outcomes for vulnerable young children who are involved in the legal and judicial systems. It develops new materials and provides training and technical assistance to improve child health-related knowledge and skills of attorneys and judges who handle cases involving young children.

Eva J. Klain, JD, is the director of Child and Adolescent Health at the ABA Center on Children and the Law. She examines legal responses to the health and developmental needs of infants and toddlers, adolescent health issues including teen pregnancy, statutory rape, domestic trafficking of children for sexual exploitation, and other issues. She has published several monographs, manuals and a bench book on criminal prosecution issues, including monographs on the prostitution of children and child sex tourism and the criminal justice system response to child pornography. Ms. Klain received her bachelor of arts degree from Cornell University and her law degree from Georgetown University.

Lisa Pilnik, JD, MS, is a staff attorney with the ABA Center on Children and the Law where she works on health issues related to court-involved infants, toddlers and preschoolers and adolescents. She also focuses on issues relating to juvenile status offenders and father involvement in the child welfare system. She has written several articles on legal and health issues related to children. Ms. Pilnik received her law degree from the University of Pennsylvania Law School and a master of science degree from the University of Pennsylvania School of Social Policy & Practice.

Erin Talati, JD, MD, earned a bachelor of arts degree at Northwestern University with majors in biology and science in human culture with honors. She subsequently graduated from the University of Pennsylvania School of Medicine with doctor of medicine and master in bioethics degrees and from the University of Pennsylvania Law School with a juris doctor degree. At Penn, she worked as a child advocate for dependent children through the Penn Legal Assistance Office. She is currently a resident physician in pediatrics at the University of Chicago Hospitals.

National Council of
Juvenile and Family Court Judges

The NCJFCJ Permanency Planning for Children Department (PPCD), directed by Nancy B. Miller, plays an essential role in working with judges to ensure that each child's case is handled swiftly and that safety, permanency, and well-being are paramount. Through national projects and initiatives, training, technical assistance, and research, the PPCD works with judges, jurisdictions and communities nationwide to implement best practices and improve outcomes for the nation's abused and neglected children and their families.

Candice L. Maze, JD, has worked for more than a decade in the child welfare arena. Ms. Maze is the president of Maze Consulting, Inc. and has directed a variety of advocacy programs and projects that interface with the juvenile court and its community partners. She has authored and coauthored a number of publications and has presented locally and nationally on topics related to children and families in the child welfare system. Ms. Maze is serving as a consultant to NCJFCJ for this project. She earned her law degree from the University of Arizona in Tucson.

Zero to Three National Policy Center

The Zero to Three Policy Center is a research-based, nonpartisan program that brings the voice of babies and toddlers to public policy at the federal, state, and community levels by translating scientific research into language that is accessible to policy makers, cultivating leadership in states and communities, and studying and sharing promising state and community strategies.

Kimberly Diamond-Berry, PhD, is a licensed clinical psychologist and a writer/training specialist for the Early Head Start National Resource Center at Zero to Three. She has developed and implemented programs for children living with chemically dependent parents in both Chicago, IL, and Washington, DC. Dr. Diamond-Berry received her doctorate in psychology from Loyola University.

Lucy Hudson, MS, is the director of the Court Teams for Maltreated Infants and Toddlers Project at Zero to Three. She has more than 30 years of experience in project management, program implementation, and policy development in public and private sector child care, child welfare, health care, and youth-serving organizations. She received her master of science degree from Wheelock College.

Index

A

AACAP (American Academy of Child and Adolescent Psychiatry), 66, 84n11, 84n17

AAP. *See* American Academy of Pediatrics

AAPD (American Academy of Pediatric Dentistry), 38, 39, 50

AAPI (Adult Adolescent Parenting Inventory), 104, 126n22

ABA (American Bar Association), Center on Children and the Law, 137

Abernethy, Pamela L., vi, x

abused and neglected very young children

    attachment disorders in, 59–63

    CAPTA/IDEA programs for, 4–5

    dental neglect, 38

    domestic violence and child abuse, 62–63

    foster care, abuse and neglect while in, 10

    lead exposure in, 28, 48

    percentage of caseload, v, 8, 9, 14n13

    poverty as most important predictor of, 76

    SBS, 47–48

    sexually transmitted infections, 29, 30

    special vulnerabilities of, vii, 8, 58

ACIP (Advisory Committee on Immunization Practices), 23–24

adoption

    disruption factors, 123–24

    foster parents, 115–16

    mediation regarding, 116

    mental health of children and, 63–65

    permanency hearings, 112–120

    postpermanency support for, 122–24

    rates for very young children, 10, 90

    TPR proceedings, 90, 115–16

    waiting for, 10

Adoption and Foster Care Analysis and Reporting System (AFCARS), 10, 14n11, 14n21, 52n33

Adoption and Safe Families Act (ASFA)

    child welfare system, 10

concurrent planning, 101-02

mental health and development needs, 75

placement of children, 90, 101, 102, 105, 116, 117, 118, 120

visitation, 105

Adult Adolescent Parenting Inventory (AAPI), 104, 126n22

Advisory Committee on Immunization Practices (ACIP), 23–24

AFCARS (Adoption and Foster Care Analysis and Reporting System), 10, 14n11, 14n21, 52n33

African-American children in care. *See also* culturally effective care, 9, 10, 37, 40

Ages & Stages Questionnaire (ASQ), 70, 108, 126n30

AIDS/HIV, 29–30, 47

Ainsworth, Mary, 83n3

alcohol abuse. *See* drug and alcohol abuse

American Academy of Child and Adolescent Psychiatry (AACAP), 66, 84n11, 84n17

American Academy of Pediatric Dentistry (AAPD), 38, 39, 50

American Academy of Pediatrics (AAP)

    assessment screenings recommended by, 21, 68

    autism-specific screenings, 60

    breastfeeding, 32n1

    culturally effective health care, 37

    guidelines for health care of children in foster care, 45

    hearing tests, 25

    HIV/AIDS screening, 30

    immunizations, 23–24

    lead screenings, 28

    medical homes, 35

    medical records for children in care, 18–19

    mental health and development needs, 84n12, 84n21–22, 86n70

    nutritional status, 33n1

    Oral Health Initiative, 41

    parasitic diseases, 31

preventive care schedule, 34, 50

SBS, 49n5

vision tests, 27

American Bar Association (ABA), Center on Children and the Law, 137

American Speech-Language-Hearing Association, 26, 27, 51n13–14

another planned permanent living arrangement (APPLA), 89, 118

anxious-ambivalent and anxious-avoidant insecure attachment, 61

APPLA (another planned permanent living arrangement), 89, 118

ASD. See autistic spectrum disorders

ASFA. See Adoption and Safe Families Act

ASQ (Ages & Stages Questionnaire), 70, 108, 126n30

assessment screenings. See also under mental health and developmental needs; physical health needs

reassessments, 108

services for parents and children, identifying, 103

asthma, 32, 35, 37, 49

attachment relationships and disorders, 59–65, 83n3

autistic spectrum disorders (ASD)

cognitive and developmental delays, 22, 65

defined, 60

indicators of, 60–61

screening for, 22, 60–61

speech and language screening, 27

vertically transmitted infections, 47

B

babbling, 26, 60

baby bottle tooth decay, 38

Bada, H. S., 62n1

Barnes, E. Whitney, 52n41, 52n49

barriers to effective health care

access issues, 44–50

cultural issues, 37

dental care, access to and awareness of, 41–44

medical homes, 36

practice tips, 17

Barth, R. P., 128n64

Battelle Developmental Inventory Screening Test (BDIST), 71

Bayley Infant Neurodevelopmental Screener (BINS), 70

BDIST (Battelle Developmental Inventory Screening Test), 71

Bellow, S. M., 85n40

BEST Oral Health Program, 41

Billings, J., 53n53

BINS (Bayley Infant Neurodevelopmental Screener), 70

birth parents. See also drug and alcohol abuse; reunification; visitation

breastfeeding by, 32

cognitive and developmental delays, 76, 117

domestic violence, 62–63, 75–76, 93

early care and education programs assisting, 81

FGC, 101, 126n16

health histories of, 18–19

HIV/AIDS screening, permission for, 30

incarcerated, 29, 106–7, 122

mental health needs of, 74–79

parenting courses for, 104–5

separation/removal of child from, 8, 58, 66, 93

services for, 74, 81, 93, 98, 103–5

sexually transmitted infections, 29, 47

TPR proceedings, 90, 115–16

vertically transmitted infections, 47

Block Grant to States, Title V Maternal and Child Health Program, 3

Block, R., 49n1

Bloomberg School of Public Health, Johns Hopkins, 61n2

Bloxcom, C., 84n5

Bodonyi, J. M., 14n23, 14n28, 14n31, 127n44, 128n63

Boger, R. P., 85n34, 85n39

Bowlby, John, 83n3

brain development/brain damage, v, vii, 47–48, 58, 62

breastfeeding, 32

Bricker, D., 126n30

Brigance Screens-II, 70–71

brothers and sisters, contact with, 73, 96, 97–98, 105, 124

Buie, J., 126n15

Burd, L., 49n2, 86n46

Buerlein, Jessie, ix, x

C

CAPTA (Child Abuse Prevention and Treatment Act), 4–5, 66, 67

Carter, S. L., 86n52

CASAs (court appointed special advocates), 92, 98, 119, 132

case handling, improving, 130, 131–33

case management, targeted (TCM), 2

case planning, 88, 100–103

CDC (Centers for Disease Control and Prevention), 14n14, 14n19, 23–24, 29, 31, 40, 61n2

Center on Children and the Law, American Bar Association (ABA), 137

Centers for Disease Control and Prevention (CDC), 14n14, 14n19, 23–24, 29, 31, 40, 61n2

CFSR (Child and Family Services Review), 90

changing and improving the child welfare system, 13, 129–35

Child Abuse Prevention and Treatment Act (CAPTA), 4–5, 66, 67

Child and Family Services Review (CFSR), 90

child care and early education, 13, 57, 80–83, 97

child-focused services, 134

Child-Parent Psychotherapy (CPP), 75–76, 78, 106, 108

Child Welfare League of America (CWLA), 45, 66, 84n11, 84n17

child welfare system, 7–14
  age as factor in experience of, 8
  case handling, improving, 130, 131–33
  changing and improving, 13, 129–35
  community-court collaborations, 130, 133–34
  cultural competence in, 91
  definition of terms, 9
  disposition of case, 88, 99–100

early experiences, importance of, 8

entry into, 9, 90

exit from, 10, 90

judges' role in, 11–12

permanency hearings, 89, 112–20

placements for children in, 13, 87–128. *See also* placement of children

preliminary protective hearings, 88, 92–98

racial statistics for children in, 9

reentry into, 11, 90

review hearings, 88–89, 107–12

Children's Defense Fund, 37n1

Children's Health Insurance Program (CHIP), 3, 43, 44

Children's Health Insurance Program Reauthorization Act (CHIPRA), 3

Christakis, D., 53n55

Chung, E., 28n1, 49n6, 51n25

CincySmiles Foundation, 41

cognitive and developmental delays
  in birth parents, 76, 117
  in children, 65–68

Cohen, Constance, x

Cohen, J., 14n10

Cohen, M., 6n4

color, children of, 9, 10, 37, 40, 79. *See also* culturally effective care

Colorado, concurrent case planning in, 102

Committee on Integrating the Science of Early Childhood Development, 62n2, 85n31, 86n48, 86n62, 86n68

communicable diseases
  immunizations against, 16, 23–24
  screening for, 29–31
  vertically transmitted infections, 47

community-court collaborations, 130, 133–34

community hospitals and centers, dental care through, 42

community leaders, judges as, 130, 132

concurrent case planning, 88, 101–3, 115

continuity/coordination of care
  dental care, 39–40
  medical care, 33–38, 45–50

141

mental health and developmental services, 71–72

practice tips, 17

Coulter, K., 49n7

court appointed special advocates (CASAs), 92, 98, 119, 132

court-based groups focusing on very young children, 132

court-involved children. *See* child welfare system

Cox, E., 50n8

CPP (Child-Parent Psychotherapy), 75–76, 78, 106, 108

culturally effective care

dependency courts, cultural competence in, 91

mental health and developmental needs, 79

permanent placements, 118

physical health needs, 37

postpermanency support for, 124

race and ethnicity, 9, 10, 37, 40, 79

Cunningham, M., 50n8

CWLA (Child Welfare League of America), 45, 66, 84n11, 84n17

D

DC:0-3 and DC:0-3R (Diagnostic Classification of Mental Health and Developmental Disorders of Infancy and Early Childhood), 59, 61n1

deafness, 24–27, 47, 49

DeLauro, L., 86n69

delays, cognitive and developmental

in birth parents, 76, 117

in children, 65–68

dental homes, 17, 39–40

dental services, 17, 38–44

dependency court. *See* child welfare system

depression, in birth parents, 74–75

developmental and cognitive delays

in birth parents, 76, 117

in children, 65–68

developmental issues generally. *See* health and developmental issues for very young children

Diagnostic Classification of Mental Health and Developmental Disorders of Infancy and Early Childhood (DC:0-3 and DC:0-3R), 59, 61n1

Diamond-Berry, Kimberly, 84n7, 138

Dicker, Sheryl, x, 50n2, 50n3, 50n7, 86n64

DiGiuseppe, D., 53n55

disabled children

IDEA Part C, 4–5, 22, 66–68

nutritional needs of, 33

disabled parents, benefits for children of, 117

disorganized attachment, 61, 63

domestic violence, 62–63, 75–76, 93

Domitrovich, Stephanie, x

Down syndrome, 25

Drinane, M., 125n9

drug and alcohol abuse

adoption, disruption of, 123–24

cognitive and developmental delays due to, 65

FASD, 46–47, 74, 76

IDEA Part C services for children exposed to, 67

importance of treating parents suffering from, 74

mental health of children living with, 61–62

neurobehavioral problems, 62

physical health of children living with, 9, 10, 29, 30, 46–47

treatment programs avoiding parent-child separation, 93, 125n10

visitation, limiting, suspending, or terminating, 111

Duncan, P. M., 33n2, 51n15, 61n4

E

ear infections

breastfeeding, 32

respiratory illnesses, 48–49

Early and Periodic Screening, Diagnosis and Treatment (EPSDT), 2–3, 24, 37, 43, 44

early care and education, 13, 57, 80–83, 97

early experiences, importance of, 8

Individual Family Services Plan (IFSP), 4

Individuals with Disabilities Education Act (IDEA) Part C, 4–5, 22, 66–68

Infant-Toddler Checklist for Language and Communication, 70

infants, health and development issues for. *See* health and developmental issues for very young children

infectious diseases. *See* communicable diseases

Institute of Medicine, 53n53, 62n2, 85n31, 86n48, 86n62, 86n68

Ippen, C. G., 86n58–61

Irving, B., 84n5

J

jail, birth parents in, 29, 106–7, 122

Jéliu, G., 127n39

Johns Hopkins Bloomberg School of Public Health, 61n2

Jones Harden, Brenda, x, 13n6, 14n8, 14n29, 84n16, 85n33, 85n35–36, 85n45, 86n47, 95, 125n1–2, 125n4, 126n13, 126n34, 127n37, 127n40, 127n42

judges' role in changing and improving child welfare, 13, 129–35

K

Karen, R., 83n4

Katz, Lynne, 86n50, 126n22

Kaye, C., 51n10

Kellogg, Anne, x

Kelly, Kay, 49n2, 86n46

Kemp, S. P., 14n23, 14n28, 14n32, 127n44, 128n63

kinship caregivers. *See* relative caregivers

Klain, Eva J., vii, 6n7, 6n10, 137

Klamath County (Oregon) Early Childhood Cavity Prevention Program, 41

Knitzer, J., 86n64

Krebs, N., 49n1

L

La Leche League International, 32

Langer, L., 125n9

language, speech, and hearing, 24–27, 47, 49, 60

Largent, B., 52n41, 52n49

Larrieu, J. A., 85n40

lead exposure, 28–29, 48

leadership, judicial, 13, 129–35

Lederman, Cindy S., x, 52n41, 52n49, 126n22

legal guardianships, 116–17, 124

legislative advocacy, 142

Lery, B., 14n15

Lester, B. M., 62n3

Lewis, M. A., 14n17

Lewis, M. L., 86n58

Lieberman, A. F., 84n8, 86n51, 86n54

Lil., Y., 52n50

Lillas, C., 125n9

limitation of visitation rights, 111

Linda Ray Intervention Center, University of Miami, 86n53

low birth weight, mental health and development affected by, 62

low-income children. *See* poverty, children living in

Lucero, Katherine, x

Lyons-Ruth, K., 85n32

M

Main, Mary, 83n3

Mallon, G. P., 126n15

malnutrition, 31–33, 46

maltreatment. *See* abused and neglected very young children

managed care plans under Medicaid, 45–50

Maternal and Child Health Block Grant to States Program, Title V, 3

Maze, Candice L., x, 138

mediation of adoption-related proceedings, 116

Medicaid, 2–3
  barriers to health care for children under, 45–50, 52n52
  children covered by, 44
  CHIP for children transitioning from, 3
  dental care, 43, 44
  EPSDT program, 2–3, 24, 37, 43, 44

medical homes, 36

postpermanency support for reunified families, 121

medical care generally. *See* mental health and developmental needs; physical health needs

medical homes, 35–36. *See also* continuity of care

medical records and health information

for comprehensive assessment screening, 21–22

confidentiality and privacy of, 4

health passports, 36–38

initial gathering of, 16, 18–20, 98

medical homes, 17, 35

practice tips, 16

mental health and developmental needs, 12–13, 55–86. *See also* autistic spectrum disorders

assessment screenings, 66–71

autism, 22, 60–61

cognitive and developmental delays, identifying, 66–68

commonly used tools, 70–71

comprehensive screening within 30 days of placement, 22, 68–69

for CPP and PCIT, 78–79

initial screening, 66

practice tips, 56

reassessments during placement, 69–71

attachment relationships and disorders, 59–65, 83n3

biological factors affecting, 62

cognitive and developmental delays

in birth parents, 76, 117

in children, 65–68

conclusions regarding, 83

continuity/coordination of services, 71–72

CPP, 75–76, 78, 106, 108

culturally effective health care, 79

diagnostic classification of common disorders, 59

early care and education, 13, 57, 80–83

factors influencing, 56, 58–65

food security, 32

FTT, 46, 64

infants, mental health disorders in, 61–62, 84n6

lead exposure, 28, 48

parents' mental health needs, 74–79

PCIT, 78–79

practice tips, 56–57

red flags, 64–65

services, providing, 56–57, 71–79, 81

sibling contact, importance of, 73

stable placements, importance of, 63–65

vertically transmitted infections, 47

visitation, as therapeutic opportunity, v, 106, 108

Miami-Dade County, FL, parenting programs in, 126n22

Miller, J. M., 128n64

Miller, Nancy B., 138

mobile dental programs, 42–43

modifications to visitation, 111–12

multiple placements, problem of, v, 8

N

National Association for the Education of Young Children, 86n67

National Center for Cultural Competence, 91

National Council of Juvenile and Family Court Judges (NCJFCJ), 39, 91, 92, 125n6–7, 131, 138. *See also RESOURCE GUIDELINES: Improving Court Practice in Child Abuse and Neglect Cases*

National Institute on Deafness and Other Communication Disorders, 51n11

National Research Council, 62n2, 85n31, 86n48, 86n62, 86n68

National Resource Center on Family Centered Practice and Permanency Planning, 127n56

Native American families and children, 79, 118

NCJFCJ (National Council of Juvenile and Family Court Judges), 39, 91, 92, 125n6–7, 131, 138. *See also RESOURCE GUIDELINES: Improving Court Practice in Child Abuse and Neglect Cases*

neglect. *See* abused and neglected very young children

neurobehavioral problems, 62

New York State Permanent Commission on Justice for Children, 45

Nicholas, S., 30n1

Nurturing Parenting Program, 78

nutrition assistance services, 31

nutritional status, 31–33, 46, 64

O

obesity, 32, 37, 64

Ohio Caseload Analysis Initiative, 85n24

Onunaku, N., 85n37

Oppenheim, D., 84n20

oral health, 17, 38–44

Osofsky, Joy D., x, 51n30, 86n52, 126n22

out-of-home care. *See* foster care

oversexualized behavior, 65

P

PANDA (Prevent Abuse and Neglect through Dental Awareness) Program, 41

parasitic diseases, 31

Parent-Child Interaction Therapy (PCIT), 78–79

parenting courses, 104–5

parents. *See also* adoption; birth parents; foster care

    resource parents, 101

Parents' Evaluation of Developmental Status (PEDS), 70

Parents' Evaluation of Developmental Status: Developmental Milestones (PEDS-DM), 70

Pawl, J. H., 86n51

PCIT (Parent-Child Interaction Therapy), 78–79

Pediatric Symptom Checklist (PSC), 71

PEDS (Parents' Evaluation of Developmental Status), 70

PEDS:DM (Parents' Evaluation of Developmental Status: Developmental Milestones), 70

permanence. *See also* reunification; adoption

    APPLA, 118

    consulting children regarding, 118–20

    extended family placements, 117

    importance of early permanence for children, v, 90

    legal guardianships, 116–17, 124

permanency hearings, 89, 112–20

    planning for permanency in placement, 92

    postpermanency support, 89, 121–24

    review hearing, assessing permanency plan in, 107–11

    timeliness of, 88, 90–92, 102

    visitation and, 106, 110

Permanency Planning for Children Department (PPCD), NCJFCJ, 138

Perry, B. D., 83n1

Persaud, D., 30n2

Pettinato, E., 52n45

PHI (protected health information) under HIPAA, 4

Phillips, D. A., 13n1–4, 14n9, 62n2, 85n31, 86n65, 86n71

physical health needs, 12, 15–53. *See also* barriers to effective care; communicable diseases; continuity/coordination of care; medical records and health information

    assessment screenings

        basic/routine screening requirements, 16, 24–32

        comprehensive assessment within 30 days of placement, 16, 21–22

        initial, 19–20

        missing information, additional screenings to obtain, 20

    conclusions regarding, 50

    dental services, 17, 38–44

    guidelines for children in foster care, 45

    hearing, speech, and language, 24–27, 47, 49

    immunizations, 16, 23–24

    lead exposure, 28–29, 48

    nutritional status, 31–33, 46

    practice tips, 16–17

    red flags, 46–49

    vision, 27, 47, 49

Pilnik, Lisa, 137

placement of children, 13, 87–128. *See also* adoption; foster care

    appropriate settings for, 93–96

    case planning, 88, 100–103

    changes in, 99

    conclusions regarding, 124–25

    consulting children regarding, 118–20

cultural competence of dependency courts and, 91

disposition of case, 88, 99–100

domestic violence cases, 76

early child care and education options, 97

extended family, 63, 93–97, 100, 116–17

family finding, 99–100, 126n14

identifying needs and services, 98–99, 103–5, 108

importance of early permanence, v, 90

legal guardianships, 116–17, 124

mental health and development, importance of stable placements to, 63–65

most-family-like setting requirement, 96, 99

multiple placements, problem of, v, 8

permanency hearings, 89, 112–20

planning for permanency in, 92

postpermanency support, 89, 121–24

practice tips, 88–89

preliminary protective hearings, 88, 92–98

review hearings, 88–89, 107–12

shelter or group care, 96, 99

support programs for caregivers, 100

timeliness requirements, 88, 90–92, 102

visitation plans, 96, 97–98, 105–7

policy advocacy, 142

poor children. *See* poverty, children living in

postpermanency support, 89, 121–24

poverty, children living in, 76

dental health, 40, 42–43

FTT, 46

lead exposure, 28, 48

PPCD (Permanency Planning for Children Department), NCJFCJ, 138

preliminary protective hearings, 88, 92–98

premature birth, 62

preschoolers, health and development issues for. *See* health and developmental issues for very young children

Prevent Abuse and Neglect through Dental Awareness (PANDA) Program, 41

preventive dental care, 39

preventive health care schedule, 34

primary relationships

early child care and education settings, 80, 82

importance of, v, 8

mental health and development, role in, 58, 59–61, 72

permanent placement requirements and, v, 90

separation/removal of child from, 8, 58, 66, 93

prison, birth parents in, 29, 106–7, 122

procedural enhancements, 134

professional groups and committees, 133

Promise Home, Tucson, AZ, 125n10

protected health information (PHI) under HIPAA, 4

PSC (Pediatric Symptom Checklist), 71

psychologial/psychiatric issues. *See* mental health and developmental needs

public education in child welfare, 132

R

race and ethnicity, 9, 10, 37, 40, 79. *See also* culturally effective care

Ratterman Baker, D., 127n47, 127n52

records. *See* medical records and health information

records, medical. *See* medical records and health information

reentry into child welfare system, 11, 90

refugee/immigrant children, 29–31

rehabilitative services, 3

relatives. *See* extended family

removal/separation, 8, 58, 66, 93

research-based reforms, 134

RESOURCE GUIDELINES: Improving Court Practice in Child Abuse and Neglect Cases, 13

endorsement of, 125n6

parental services, identifying, 98

on placement of very young children, 92

resource parents, 101

respiratory illnesses, 48–49

reunification
  case planning and, 100, 101
  at disposition of case, 99
  extending timeframe for, 120
  permanency hearings, 113–14, 120
  postpermanency support for, 121–22
  rates for very young children, 10, 90
  review hearings, 108–9
  short-term effects of, 114
  transition planning for, 114
  visitation and, 105–6
review hearings, 88–89, 107–12
Robinson, S. D., 126n17–18

S

safety net providers of dental care, 42–44, 53n53
SAMHSA (Substance Abuse and Mental Health Services Administration), 77–78
San Mateo County, CA, concurrent case planning in, 102–3
Santucci, R., 67n2
Savage, M. F., 52n43
SBS (shaken baby syndrome), 47–48
Schechter, S., 85n44
school-based centers, dental care through, 42
Schuder, M. R., 85n32
Schumacher, R., 86n69
Seale, N., 52n45
secure attachment, 59–61
separation/removal, 8, 58, 66, 93
SESBI-R (Sutter Eyberg Student Behavior Inventory Revised), 71
sexual abuse, 29, 30
sexualized behavior in very young children, 65
sexually transmitted infections, 29, 47
shaken baby syndrome (SBS), 47–48
Shaw, J. S., 33n2, 51n15, 61n4
shelter or group care, 96, 99, 118
Shonkoff, J. P., 13n1–4, 14n9, 62n2, 85n31, 86n65, 86n71
sibling contact, 73, 96, 97–98, 105, 124
Siegel, D., 84n10

sight, assessment and care of, 27, 47, 49
Silverman, R., 86n51
Simon, N. P., 49n4
Sinclair, S. A., 52n44
sisters and brothers, contact with, 73, 96, 97–98, 105, 124
small for gestational age infants, mental health and development of, 62
Smariga, Margaret, 84n19, 106, 126n11, 126n23–26, 126n31
Smith, A. B., 85n34, 85n39
Smith, P. K., 71
social-emotional development. *See* mental health and developmental needs
social indicators of autism spectrum disorders (ASD), 60
Social Security Act, Title IV-E, 2, 44, 117, 118
Sofka, D., 52n31
Solchany, JoAnne, x
Sommers, A., 6n4–5
Special Supplemental Nutrition Program for Women, Infants and Children (WIC), 31
speech, hearing, and language, 24–27, 47, 49, 60
Squires, J., 126n30
states. *See also* Medicaid
  dental care programs, 41, 42
  hearing evaluations for newborns, 25, 51n10
  Title V Maternal and Child Health Block Grant to States Program, 3
Story, M., 52n31
Strengthening Families Program, 77
substance abuse. *See* drug and alcohol abuse
Substance Abuse and Mental Health Services Administration (SAMHSA), 77–78
support programs for caregivers, 100
suspension of visitation rights, 111
Sutter Eyberg Student Behavior Inventory Revised (SESBI-R), 71
syphilis, 29, 47
Szilagyi, Moira, ix, 34

T

Takayama, J., 49n7

Talati, Erin, 137

TANF (Temporary Aid to Needy Families), 121

targeted case management (TCM), 2

Tartar, R. E., 83–84n5

TB (tuberculosis), 29–31

TCM (targeted case management), 2

teeth, caring for, 38–44

Temporary Aid to Needy Families (TANF), 121

termination of parental rights (TPR) proceedings, 90, 115–16

termination of visitation rights, 111

Title IV-E, Social Security Act, 2, 44, 117, 118

Title V Maternal and Child Health Block Grant to States Program, 3

toddlers, health and development issues for. *See* health and developmental issues for very young children

Towey, Kelly, x

TPR (termination of parental rights) proceedings, 90, 115–16

training programs as dental care safety nets, 43

Treacher Collins syndrome, 25

tuberculosis (TB), 29–31

U

University of Miami Linda Ray Intervention Center, 86n53

Usher syndrome, 25

V

vaccinations, 16, 23–24

Vandell, D. L., 86n66

vertically transmitted infections, 47

very young children, health and development issues for. *See* health and developmental issues for very young children

The Village South, Miami, FL, 125n10

vision assessment and care, 27, 47, 49

visitation, 105–7

   alternative terms for, 106

   breastfeeding, 32

   in child care and education settings, 82

   distress of child following, 73

   limiting, suspending, or terminating, 111

   mental health of child and, 72–73

   modifications to, 111–12

   permanency goals and, 106, 110

   placement arrangements and, 96, 97–98, 105–7

   reunification, supporting, 105–6

   review hearings, 110–12

   sibling contact, 73, 96, 97–98, 105, 124

   as therapeutic opportunity, v, 106, 108

W

Wang, W., 52n50

Wanlass, J., 84n20

Webb, D., 28n1

Webb, M., 52n45

Weinick, R. M., 53n53

Whitbeck, L. B., 84n5

WIC (Women, Infants and Children), 31, 42

Wolfe, B., 86n66

Wolfe, E., 49n7

Women, Infants and Children (WIC), 31, 42

Wright, Lois E., 85n26–27, 85n29

Wulczyn, F., 13n6, 14n8, 14n15–16, 14n20, 14n24–27, 14n30–31, 125n1, 127n62

Y

Youcha, V., 14n10

Z

Zeanah, C. H., 84n6

Zero to Three National Policy Center, 59, 138